Tableau for Business Users

Learn to Automate and Simplify Dashboards for Better Decision Making

Shankar Arul

Apress®

Tableau for Business Users: Learn to Automate and Simplify Dashboards for Better Decision Making

Shankar Arul
Montreuil, France

ISBN-13 (pbk): 978-1-4842-7785-0   ISBN-13 (electronic): 978-1-4842-7786-7
https://doi.org/10.1007/978-1-4842-7786-7

Managing Director, Apress Media LLC: Welmoed Spahr
Acquisitions Editor: Aditee Mirashi
Coordinating Editor: Mark Powers

Cover designed by eStudioCalamar

Cover image by Felix Dubois on Unsplash (www.unsplash.com)

Distributed to the book trade worldwide by Apress Media, LLC, 1 New York Plaza, New York, NY 10004, U.S.A. Phone 1-800-SPRINGER, fax (201) 348-4505, e-mail orders-ny@springer-sbm.com, or visit www.springeronline.com. Apress Media, LLC is a California LLC and the sole member (owner) is Springer Science + Business Media Finance Inc (SSBM Finance Inc). SSBM Finance Inc is a **Delaware** corporation.

For information on translations, please e-mail booktranslations@springernature.com; for reprint, paperback, or audio rights, please e-mail bookpermissions@springernature.com.

Apress titles may be purchased in bulk for academic, corporate, or promotional use. eBook versions and licenses are also available for most titles. For more information, reference our Print and eBook Bulk Sales web page at http://www.apress.com/bulk-sales.

Any source code or other supplementary material referenced by the author in this book is available to readers on GitHub via the book's product page, located at www.apress.com/9781484277850. For more detailed information, please visit http://www.apress.com/source-code.

Printed on acid-free paper

Table of Contents

About the Author

Shankar Arul has a master's degree in industrial engineering from Virginia Tech and an MBA in finance from ESSEC Business School in France. He has more than 15 years of hands-on experience in data visualization and data science. Having faced the frustrations of business users with data-driven decision-making in companies like BNP, Apple, Groupon, and Kering, he decided to enable business users with the power of data visualization and Tableau through this book.

About the Technical Reviewer

 **Ashwini Potdar** is a senior Tableau developer at Onit, engaged in developing, maintaining and managing pre-packaged and custom BI systems on Tableau software for multiple law and consulting firms. With 7 plus years of experience working in various domains, she brings immense value to the table by turning raw, unorganized and huge data sets into actionable information.

Testimonial

In the age of big data, small businesses and large corporations need to rely on data analytics for their day-to-day decisions and strategic orientations. This book provides an easy approach to quickly master data visualization using Tableau, allowing you to make clear and efficient choices.

—Ait Voncke, CEO, Aviv Group

Acknowledgments

As always, I would like to thank my parents, who enabled me to write this book in the first place, and my wife, who supports me in all my endeavors. I would also like to make a special dedication to my kids Nikie and Brooklyn, who show me the joy of life every day. Special thanks to Santosh Arul for his help with Photoshop. You can reach him at sarul.design@gmail.com for your Photoshop and Illustrator design needs.

Introduction

My goal with this book is to help business users learn how to use Tableau for data analytics and visualization. Business users have plenty of questions to answer to run their business effectively. Unfortunately, they do not possess the right tools or the skillset to query the data which holds the answers to these questions. *Tableau for Business Users* is geared towards "data novice" business users and will help you master Tableau by walking you through concrete examples and issues that you might face in your day-to-day work.

Over the course of the book, I'll also distill the core of Tableau into a few concepts. From there, it's just a matter of combining them in many different ways to build whatever data visualizations and analyses you need. Starting from the fundamentals of data, this book gently builds up the pace by introducing you to the crux of Tableau, the subtleties of authoring calculated fields, and Tableau calculations, all the way up to advanced functionalities such as level of detail calculations. I bring everything together in a chapter on dashboarding, helping you build actionable dashboards to effectively communicate your analysis and visualizations.

Data-driven decision-making is no longer a "nice to have" in today's context, but an absolute must. This book will prepare you to tackle the challenges of big data and data analytics by helping you to master Tableau without getting bogged down in the technicalities of the tool. Excel, which is the go-to tool for any competent business professional, needs to be complemented by a data visualization tool such as Tableau to help effectively communicate and share your findings. This book will help you in this transition to the era of big data.

CHAPTER 1

Why Visualize Data?

Over the past few decades, Microsoft Excel has become the de facto data analytics tool for most business users. When you need the sum of two values, it couldn't be simpler than clicking the first value you need to add, following it up with a + sign, and adding the next value. Voilà! You have a total of two values. Drag the formula down by clicking the corners. You've got a sum of two columns.

Unfortunately, this flexibility comes at a cost. The user gets gradually trapped in the world of quick fixes and patched formulas that Excel offers. Initially, Lotus 123, the predecessor of Excel, was conceived primarily as a data entry tool, and indeed, Excel *excels* at this task.

But now, in this new era of big data, data visualization and data analytics require their own toolkit. The human brain does a very poor job deciphering meaningful trends from a table of raw data (numbers), but at the same time excels at comparing, extrapolating, and spotting trends in visual shapes and colors. It turns out the brain can take in a picture and process it in one stroke while linearly processing text. Imagine a bar chart that condenses 100 rows of data into a few columns against reading the rows one by one. You start to get the picture. It's the responsibility of the analyst to effectively distill and convey the meaning hidden behind the numbers through effective and meaningful visualizations.

© Shankar Arul 2022
S. Arul, *Tableau for Business Users*, https://doi.org/10.1007/978-1-4842-7786-7_1

If you take a close look at the raw numbers shown in Figure 1-1, you can make a few observations.

- There are four data sets.

- Each data set has an x and y column.

- Numbers seem to range from 4 to 13.

- There are at most two decimals.

Anscombe's quartet

I		II		III		IV	
x	y	x	y	x	y	x	y
10.0	8.04	10.0	9.14	10.0	7.46	8.0	6.58
8.0	6.95	8.0	8.14	8.0	6.77	8.0	5.76
13.0	7.58	13.0	8.74	13.0	12.74	8.0	7.71
9.0	8.81	9.0	8.77	9.0	7.11	8.0	8.84
11.0	8.33	11.0	9.26	11.0	7.81	8.0	8.47
14.0	9.96	14.0	8.10	14.0	8.84	8.0	7.04
6.0	7.24	6.0	6.13	6.0	6.08	8.0	5.25
4.0	4.26	4.0	3.10	4.0	5.39	19.0	12.50
12.0	10.84	12.0	9.13	12.0	8.15	8.0	5.56
7.0	4.82	7.0	7.26	7.0	6.42	8.0	7.91
5.0	5.68	5.0	4.74	5.0	5.73	8.0	6.89

Figure 1-1. *Anscombe's data set*

Squeeze your eyelids together to squeeze out more information from this table. The more astute among you might have copied and pasted these numbers into a good ol' Excel sheet and grabbed your "I'm a data scientist" coffee mug. Then, you start making a list.

- Average of x: 9

- Sample variance of x: 11

- Average of y: 7.5

- Sample variance of x: 4.125

- Correlation between x and y: 0.816

- A nice linear regression line: $y = 3 + 0.5x$

- R2 of the linear regression line: 0.67

That's a lot of numbers. The strange thing you notice is that this list is the same across the four data sets. It's easy to make fairly simplistic reductions about the distributions of x and y that they are similar based on the summary statistics. A quick visualization is shown in Figure 1-2.

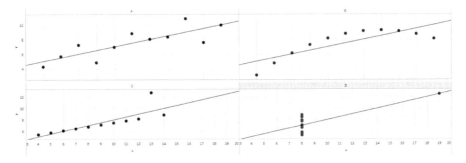

Figure 1-2. *Anscombe's data set in Tableau*

The hidden gems in the distributions are instantly revealed. This example also helps underline the importance of exploratory data analytics before drawing any inferences and conclusions.

I'm certainly not discouraging the use of Excel in any way. It's a powerful tool in the repertoire of any competent professional. The main point I want to drive home is that Excel often needs to be complemented by a data visualization tool to help effectively communicate and share your findings. This is where Tableau steps in to help you share your analyses through compelling visualizations.

1.1 Who This Book Is For

The audience for this book includes business analysts, data analysts, and financial analysts, and anyone who is hitting the limits of Excel for their data analytics needs. If your day-to-day work involves staring at numbers all day, then you're part of the target audience. There are no prerequisites to follow the concepts in this book. You work your way gradually from the very fundamentals of data all the way up to building fancy dashboards and visualizations based on gigabytes of data.

1.2 How Is This Book Different?

There are many Tableau user guides and reference manuals that do an excellent job presenting every menu, tab, button, pane, and shelf in Tableau. If you're the kind of person who needs to know every single button and functionality tucked into Tableau, then this might not be the right book for you.

When you start to learn a new language and want to go about it systematically and methodically, you start with the grammar. Understanding the foundational underpinnings of a language helps you get the basics right, and then it's a matter of stringing words together to make sentences. A logical next step is to line up words within the rules defined by the grammar (or not) in infinite ways—to write Shakespearean poetry or tabloid articles, or to have conversations.

This book intends to approach the subject of mastering Tableau in a similar fashion. I'll try to distill the very core of Tableau in a few concepts, and then it's just a matter of combining them in infinite possible ways to build the required data visualizations.

1.3 How to Contact Us

Please address comments and questions concerning this book to tableau-the-book@jupyterdata.com. If you need any help on your data analytics projects, please feel free to reach out at shankar.arul@jupyterdata.com. You can also find me on LinkedIn.

1.4 Summary

This chapter discussed how visualizations can complement your numerical analysis and how Tableau can help you better communicate your analyses and data insights. The next chapter explains how to install Tableau on your computer and set up a Tableau profile where you can save your analyses on Tableau's public cloud for free.

CHAPTER 2

Installation and Setup

This chapter succinctly explains the installation of Tableau Public, which is used in this book. Unfortunately, if you work on macOS or Linux, I'll have to redirect your questions and concerns to the almighty Google.

Head over to Tableau Public's site at `https://public.tableau.com/en-us/s/` (see Figure 2-1). Hand over your email, as usual, in return for the Tableau Public installation file (.exe).

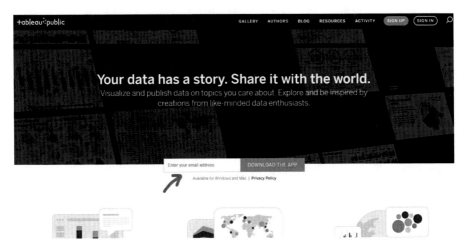

Figure 2-1. *Tableau Public download page*

Double-click the .exe and follow the instructions to complete the installation of Tableau Public.

We're using Tableau Public version 2021.2 for the various examples illustrated in this book. You should be fairly safe using newer versions of Tableau Public without running into backward compatibility issues.

© Shankar Arul 2022
S. Arul, *Tableau for Business Users*, https://doi.org/10.1007/978-1-4842-7786-7_2

But do keep in mind (at least since 2019) that Tableau has been releasing one major version a year, including some minor revisions. For example, after the launch of Tableau version 2020, there were four incremental updates, ending with Tableau 2020.4 by December.

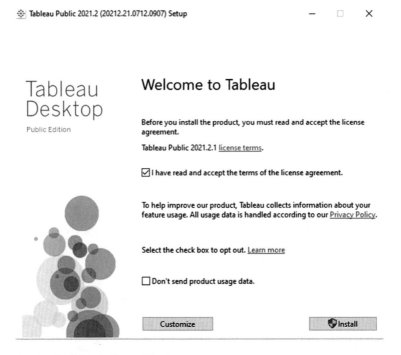

Figure 2-2. *Tableau Installation screen*

You can also create your own profile page on Tableau Public's website. This helps you save your dashboards on your Tableau Public profile page and eventually share them with other Tableau users. You can either choose to simply allow users to visualize and interact with your dashboards or even allow them to download the original Tableau workbook powering the dashboards, which they can play with and modify. As of September 2021, Tableau provides 10 GB of free storage space to upload your data sets and dashboards.

It's time to take the cover off and take Tableau for a quick spin. As soon as you open Tableau, click Microsoft Excel under Connect, as shown in Figure 2-3.

Figure 2-3. *Tableau connects to Excel*

On the next screen, drag and drop the Excel tab from which you'd like to import the data, as shown in Figure 2-4. The Preview pane gives you a quick overview of the data that was imported. Head over to the Sheet 1 tab (highlighted in Figure 2-4), where you build visualizations in the coming chapters.

Figure 2-4. *Tableau imports data from tab*

2.1 Data Sources Required for the Exercises in the Book

The various Tableau workbooks, Excel files, and CSV files you need to follow along are available on this book's GitHub source page at https:// github.com/shankararul/tableau_for_business_users. You can also directly get the workbooks from the Tableau Public server available under my profile.

2.2 Summary

This chapter explained how to install Tableau 2021.2 Public and set up a free Tableau Public profile where you can save your analysis. The next chapter briefly looks at the fundamentals of data and a structured way of converting your business questions to the language of data.

CHAPTER 3

Fundamentals of Data

Now that the formalities of setting up Tableau are done, let's step into the shallow end of the pool with some basic data types. Essentially, you can broadly categorize any piece of data into the following three types.

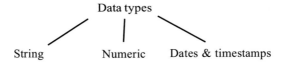

Nothing mind-blowing so far.

The following are a few business-oriented examples.

- **String/textual** data types include product names, categories, and so forth (identified by the Abc next to column names in Tableau).

- **Geographic** data types (typically textual) include country, city, or postal code (identified by the globe icon).

- **Numeric** data types include profit, sales, sale price, and so forth (identified by the # icon).

- **Date types** include invoice date, shipping date, return time, and so forth (identified by the calendar icon).

You have the flexibility to change the data types if Tableau doesn't interpret the data type correctly. For example, the Row ID column is

© Shankar Arul 2022
S. Arul, *Tableau for Business Users*, https://doi.org/10.1007/978-1-4842-7786-7_3

interpreted as a number that must be changed into a string. Click the **123** icon next to the column name and switch it to the string datatype. This transformation of data types can be done directly in any of the sheets (as highlighted in Figure 3-1) or in the Preview section of the **Data Source** pane by clicking the icons above the column names.

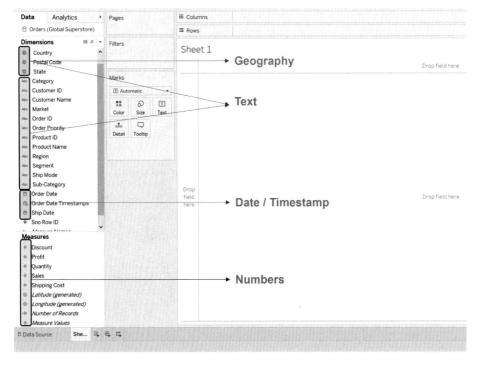

Figure 3-1. *Data types in Tableau*

You should also have noticed that the numeric columns are arranged at the bottom of the screen under the **Measures** pane, and the string/textual, date-time column types are arranged at the top under the **Dimensions** pane. This is based on how Tableau considers and treats these data types as either continuous or discrete quantities.

In addition to classifying data types based on their intrinsic value, you could classify them based on continuity in the values. For example, the product names are discrete values. In the superstore data set, you'll notice three types of values in the category column: Furniture, Office Supplies, and Technology. There is no sense of continuity between the three distinct values, so they are called *discrete values*.

⚡ DIMENSIONS AND MEASURES (WORKS ONLY IN DESKTOP EDITIONS >= VERSIONS 2021)

You can quickly filter the columns by type using the following shortcuts.

"D:" displays only the dimensions. (D followed by the colon symbol)

"M:" displays only the measures.

"C:" displays only the calculated fields you create in Tableau.

On the other hand, take the example of the order date column, which contains dates. When you want to understand the sales over the past three years of order dates, consider the Date column as a continuous range as the days are in successive order, and you want to see the evolution across time.

⚡ DISCRETE VS. CONTINUOUS QUANTITIES

Discrete columns are identified in blue pills, and *continuous quantities* are identified as green pills. This subtle difference often leads to "unexpected outcomes" in visualizations.

You can switch the variable type from discrete to continuous or vice versa, and there are many ways of doing it. For example, you could right-click the YEAR(Order Date) green pill as shown in Figure 3-2 and switch it to discrete. This ensures that this value is treated as a discrete value in this analysis.

Figure 3-2. *Discrete vs. continuous data types*

The four most common ways to aggregate the measures (numeric columns) are SUM, MIN, MAX, AVG. You'll find them by right-clicking the green numeric pills and hovering over the **Measure** submenu. You can calculate the median, variances, and standard deviations in the same submenu. Aggregations are not constrained to measures. You can also aggregate the dimensions to either count the values or count the distinct values. For example, you can count the product ID to calculate the total number of products/items or count the distinct number of products sold by choosing the **Count (Distinct)** option.

3.1 Data Sources

To start building your visualizations with Tableau, you need to first import some data. Let's walk through these steps with Excel and CSV files. Section 5.4 shows how to bring in more than one data source because you might have data coming in from multiple sources. For example, you need to consolidate budget data from the finance team, sales data from Salesforce, and web performance data from Google Analytics in your reports. Let's build slowly to that, starting with a single data source in this section.

There are three tabs in the Global Superstore .xlsx file: **Orders**, **Returns**, and **People**. The **Orders** tab was imported in section 2.1.

I want to draw your attention to a few points in this step.

By default, when Tableau imports data, it previews the first few rows in a tabular format (see Figure 3-3). If you prefer to see the list of columns to make sure that they imported properly and that their data types were inferred properly, you can switch views by clicking the **Manage metadata** icon (see highlighted box 1 in Figure 3-3). This provides the metadata shown in Figure 3-4. In addition, you can give the column names an alias. For example, suppose you want to change the column name from Row ID to Sno Row. In that case, you would change the value under the **Field Name** column. These aliases replace your column names everywhere in your Tableau reports.

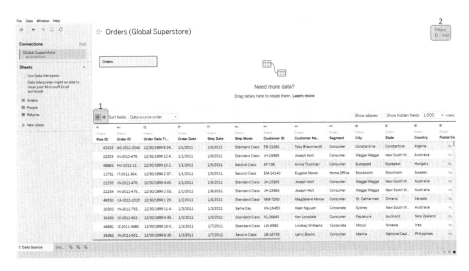

Figure 3-3. *Excel data import*

Field Name	Table	Remote Field Name
# Row ID	Orders	Row ID
Abc Order ID	Orders	Order ID
Order Date Timestamps	Orders	Order Date Timestamps
Order Date	Orders	Order Date
Ship Date	Orders	Ship Date
Abc Ship Mode	Orders	Ship Mode
Abc Customer ID	Orders	Customer ID
Abc Customer Name	Orders	Customer Name
Abc Segment	Orders	Segment
City	Orders	City
State	Orders	State
Country	Orders	Country
Postal Code	Orders	Postal Code
Abc Market	Orders	Market
Abc Region	Orders	Region
Abc Product ID	Orders	Product ID
Abc Category	Orders	Category

Figure 3-4. Excel metadata

Data source filters could also be interesting to you at this step. For example, let's say you're responsible for the French sales, and you want to import only the data where the Country column is equal to France. You could add a global data source filter that filters the data upstream before getting imported into Tableau. Clicking **Add** next to the filters (see the highlighted box 2 in Figure 3-3) lets you go through the steps illustrated in Figure 3-5.

16

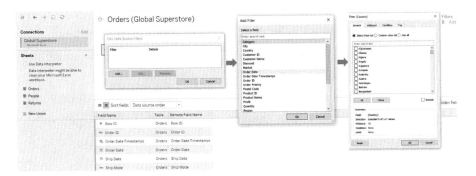

Figure 3-5. *Data source filters*

✈ EXTRACT VS. LIVE DATA?

When you work with SQL-like data sources, you've got two ways of working
with data. You could work in Live mode, in which the data is queried in real
time by Tableau (e.g., every time you build a visualization for your report). On
the other hand, if you select Extract mode, Tableau pulls down the data and
stores it locally in .hyper format on your computer. As a result, subsequent
querying and processing are much faster compared to the Live mode.

In case you're working with voluminous data, it's recommended to put the
data source in Extract mode to help you keep things fluid while you slice and
dice the data. Section 7.7 goes into more detail.

3.2 Data Preparation

You would have probably heard analysts working with a lot of data gripe
that 80% of their time is spent cleaning and preparing data. Unfortunately,
it is no exaggeration. I would even push it up to 90–95%. A vast suite of
tools can help you get data in the right format for your analysis, such
as Alteryx and Tableau Data Prep. Excel VBA can be very helpful when

you want to perform certain manual actions in your Excel files. Data preparation is a topic that merits its own stand-alone book. But data analytics solutions work best on tabular data in which each row presents a unique combination of values.

Table 3-1 provides a classical tabular data set of profits by country and segment. For example, Australia repeats twice (one row when segment = Home Office and one when segment = Consumer). The sum of profits across all countries and segments is $62,000.

Table 3-1. *Tabular Data*

Country	Segment	Profit
Algeria	Consumer	$9,000
Australia	Home Office	$5,000
Hungary	Corporate	$7,000
Sweden	Home Office	$9,000
Canada	Corporate	$10,000
Australia	Consumer	$5,000
Hungary	Consumer	$3,000
Canada	Home Office	$9,000
Sweden	Consumer	$5,000
		$62,000

The same values can be represented in a pivoted fashion, as illustrated in Table 3-2. The pivoted data set manages to provide the same values in a more condensed format. Unfortunately, this data set would not work as well as the tabular data set with any data analytics tool. You need to transpose the three segments in the column headers into a new column called segment to return your initial tabular data set. This operation goes by many names, including *transpose, stack,* and *pivot.*

Table 3-2. *Pivoted Data*

Country / Segment	Consumer	Home Office	Corporate	Profit by Country
Algeria	$9,000	$0	$0	$9,000
Australia	$5,000	$5,000	$0	$10,000
Hungary	$3,000	$0	$7,000	$10,000
Sweden	$5,000	$9,000	$0	$14,000
Canada	$0	$9,000	$10,000	$19,000
Profit by Segment >	$22,000	$23,000	$17,000	**$62,000**

Let's say you've got a table of sales across the last 12 months for five countries in a pivoted data format. You can easily transform this data into a tabular version in Tableau. First, import the Excel file (see the Chapter 3 Transpose tab in the Global Superstore data set available on GitHub) into Tableau, and then select the 12 months of data, keeping the Shift key pressed. Next, right-click the column and then click **Pivot**, as highlighted in Figure 3-6. This creates your tabular data set on which you can easily start comparing MoM (Month over Month), QoQ (Quarter over Quarter) comparisons which are discussed in later chapters.

Table 3-3. Monthly Sales Data

Country	01-Jan-20	01-Feb-20	01-Mar-20	01-Apr-20	01-May-20	01-Jun-20	01-Jul-20	01-Aug-20	01-Sep-20	01-Oct-20	01-Nov-20	01-Dec-20
Algeria	$7,000	$9,000	$1,000	$4,000	$6,000	$8,000	$8,000	$5,000	$2,000	$3,000	$3,000	$1,000
Australia	$1,000	$9,000	$2,000	$3,000	$4,000	$3,000	$10,000	$5,000	$10,000	$4,000	$7,000	$8,000
Hungary	$2,000	$2,000	$9,000	$10,000	$5,000	$5,000	$8,000	$3,000	$10,000	$1,000	$1,000	$8,000
Sweden	$8,000	$10,000	$9,000	$6,000	$8,000	$8,000	$1,000	$3,000	$10,000	$10,000	$6,000	$2,000
Canada	$10,000	$9,000	$7,000	$7,000	$2,000	$3,000	$3,000	$8,000	$1,000	$1,000	$6,000	$9,000

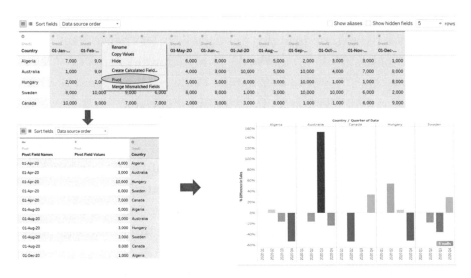

Figure 3-6. *Pivot data in Tableau*

✈ AVAILABILITY OF PIVOT OPTION?

The Pivot option is not supported on all data sources. It works when you use a single Microsoft Excel file, text file, Google Sheets file, or PDF as a data source. Otherwise, you might have to use a custom SQL to make the Pivot option available on other data sources.

3.3 Converting Business Questions to the Language of Data

> *The wise man doesn't give the right answers. He poses the right questions.*
>
> —Claude Levi-Strauss

When the questions are asked in the right format, the answers eventually reveal themselves.

So far, you have managed to import data into Tableau, and now the logical next step is to start analyzing this data. First, let's pause for a second and make sure that you have the right framework to ask the "right" business questions. The word *right* applies to the validity of the syntax of the question, not the legitimacy of your business question.

Let's say you want to visualize the profit generated by Qatar in the last three months for every category of product sold. The recommended way to gently rephrase the question is as follows: **Total Profit** by **Category** when **Order Date** <=3 months and **Country** is equal to **Qatar**.

Start with the value you want to measure (appropriately called a *measure* in Tableau) and how you want to aggregate this measure (average or sum, or minimum or maximum, etc.).

This is followed by the variable that you want to break down this measure by. In this example, it is by category of product. This variable is called a *dimension*. You can follow this up with as many dimensions as you want. But unfortunately, as soon as you add more than two dimensions to a chart, the visualizations tend to get much more complicated and harder to infer.

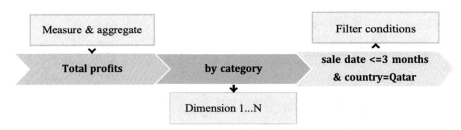

Let's do another example. This time let's calculate the unique number of orders by country for each subcategory in the office supplies category.

Count distinct (Order ids)	by country & sub category	category=office supplies

If you wanted to analyze the year-over-year (YoY) % growth (order date) of the unique orders that you calculated, the entire reformulated question would read as such.

Let's start with the distinct count of order IDs broken down by country and subcategory with a filter on the **Category** column set to **Office Supplies**. Once you answer this question, you need to calculate the percentage difference across these values, grouped by the order date–year dimension.

3.4 Summary

This chapter covered the fundamentals of data along with the various data types. You saw how to import the data and get it in the right format suited for analysis. You also saw an easy framework that allows you to convert business questions in the right structure and then easily transpose them onto Tableau. The focus of the next chapter is building visualizations and understanding the foundational underpinnings of Tableau.

CHAPTER 4

The Crux of Tableau

By now, you should have a fair understanding of how to import data into Tableau and ensure that the data types have been properly inferred. You should also know the basic semantics of converting business questions into the language of data analytics. Now that the foundation is set, it's time to look at the crux of Tableau—the four building blocks that create and refine your data visualizations.

4.1 Dimensions, Measures, and Aggregations

You know what dimensions, measures, and aggregations mean in the context of data analytics. I noticed that in the paid version of Tableau (Tableau Desktop), dimensions and measures are appropriately highlighted, unlike in Tableau Public, which is the free version. I'm guessing the $70 license fee buys a few nice-looking labels in addition to many other functionalities.

The continuous quantities highlighted in green (measures) are aggregated and broken down or not by dimensions (see Figure 4-1). You could take a non-continuous quantity, such as user ID, and aggregate it (count or unique) to make it a measure.

© Shankar Arul 2022
S. Arul, *Tableau for Business Users*, https://doi.org/10.1007/978-1-4842-7786-7_4

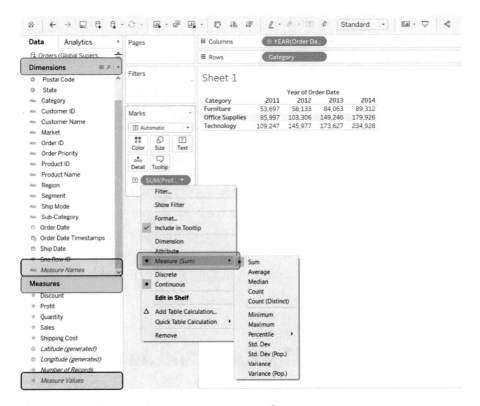

Figure 4-1. *Dimensions, measures, and aggregates*

If you scroll to the bottom of each shelf in the dimensions and Measures shelf, you'll see the two fields measure names, and the values tucked in. Unfortunately, most Tableau beginners fail to notice these two columns that offer a lot of flexibility to your analysis. You'll extensively use these two columns in Chapter 6.

By default, when you drag and drop your measures, Tableau aggregates them as a sum. This is usually handy, but let's say you have a column containing a ratio, and you always need to average the values instead of summing them. You can change the default aggregation measures to an average, for example, as highlighted in Figure 4-2 by right-clicking the measure.

Figure 4-2. *Set default aggregations for measures*

→A USE-CASE FOR MEASURE NAMES AND MEASURE VALUES

In this unrealistic use-case, let's say you want to pile up discounts, profits, and sales in a bar chart. If you try dragging the three measures into the Rows shelf, you'll end up getting three discrete bars in blue on the right, as shown in Figure 4-3. But instead, if you drop measure values on the Rows shelf and measure names in the Filters shelf, you can pile them up on top of each other (as highlighted on the left).

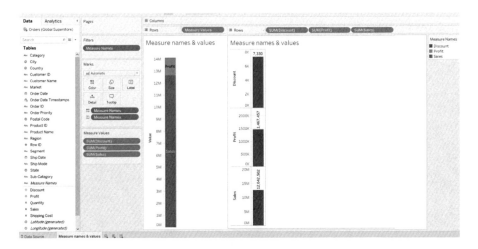

Figure 4-3. *Measures names and values*

4.2 Columns and Rows Shelves

To illustrate the use of the Columns and Rows shelves in Tableau, let's go back to the basic terminology of a bar chart as illustrated in Figure 4-4. In the case of this bar chart, the Columns shelf houses the dimension, which is a category in this example. As a result, there are three vertical columns (Furniture, Office Supplies, and Technology). Similarly, the Rows shelf houses **Measure total profits**. As a result, on the y-axis, the total profits determine the heights of the vertical bars. To hammer the point home, what would the result be if you were to swap the pills in Rows and Columns shelves (i.e., SUM(Profit) in the Columns shelf and Category in the Rows shelf)? This is illustrated in Figure 4-5.

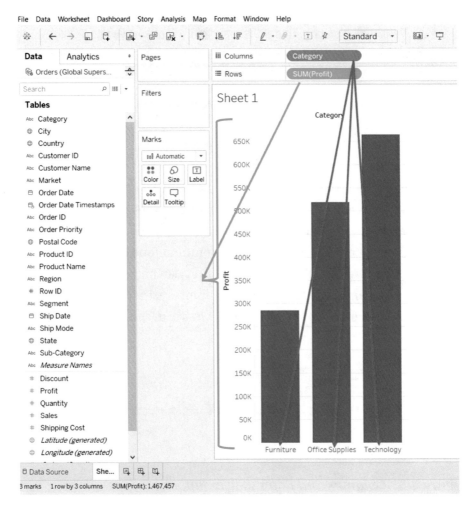

Figure 4-4. *Bar chart*

⚡ DO YOU ALWAYS NEED THE ROWS AND COLUMN SHELVES?

It turns out that you don't need to use the Rows and Columns shelves in all your visualizations. For example, with treemaps, pie charts, or packed bubbles, you can completely do away with the concept of rows and columns. Do you see why? If not, don't worry. This is the topic that you deep dive into in the next section.

You have the flexibility to pile up the dimensions and measures in the Columns or Rows shelves. For example, let's say you drop in the year of order date in addition to the category along the Columns shelf, you should see the visualization as in Figure 4-6.

Since there are three unique categories and four years of order history, can you predict the number of bars in the graph? 12! Each product category gets broken down by the order year, and hence 3 * 4 = 12. The Cartesian product pours through various combinations very quickly to spot outliers and trends. If rightly applied, they can be very helpful in your exploratory data analysis. But as a rule of thumb, restrict yourself to less than two dimensions in your visualizations in the dashboards.

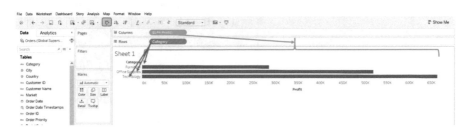

Figure 4-5. *Columns and Rows shelves flipped horizontal bar*

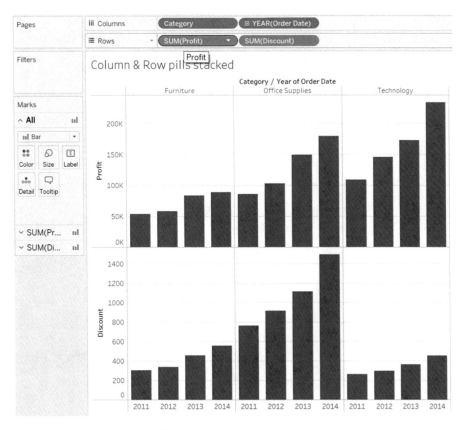

Figure 4-6. *Stacking the Columns and Rows shelves*

4.3 Marks Card

Armed with the knowledge of the first two building blocks, you can start unleashing bar charts, horizontal bar charts, line charts, and many other visualizations. The next challenge is to change the color of the charts or increase the size of the elements in the visualization or show labels and tooltips on your visualizations to make them striking. This is where the Marks section comes in handy.

The Marks card (highlighted in Figure 4-7) is composed of two main blocks. The orange is a drop-down that lets you play around with the shape of the visualization. The blue block is composed of six subblocks that help you customize the various visual elements in a graph. Let's start with the blue block and get to the visualization type (orange block) later.

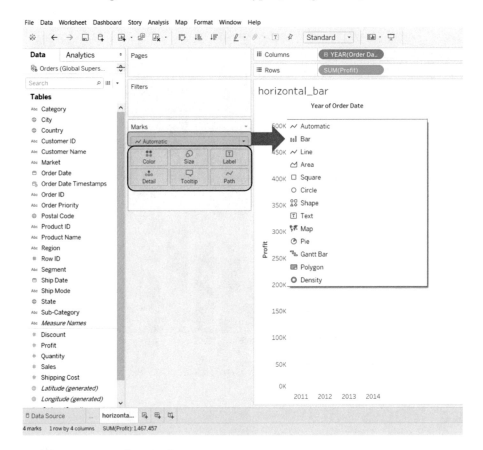

Figure 4-7. *Marks card*

4.3.1 Color Block

The Color block allows you to change the colors of the graphical elements. There are two ways to use this functionality. First, you could use it to change the color of the graph. When you click it directly, you get a pop-up that looks like what's shown in Figure 4-8. You can also add corporate color codes to your custom color palette to save some time.

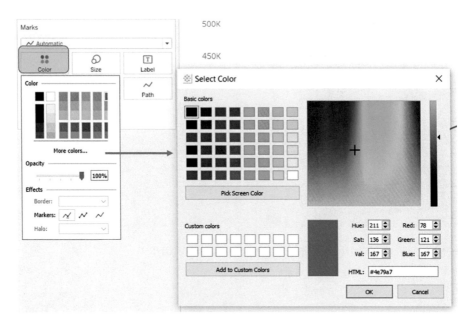

Figure 4-8. *Option 1: Change colors*

The second and more interesting approach is by dropping in a dimension into the color box. This breaks down the visualization into a more granular, detailed visualization by associating each unique value in the dimension with color. Figure 4-9 shows how the line chart gets broken into three distinct lines for each category. This lets you see how each category performed with respect to each other across the years in terms of profit.

I want to draw your attention to a subtle but evident point of the result you get while you drop the category dimension in the Columns shelf along with the year, as illustrated in Figure 4-9.

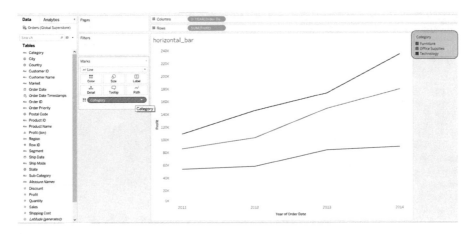

Figure 4-9. *Option 2: Breakdown by dimensions*

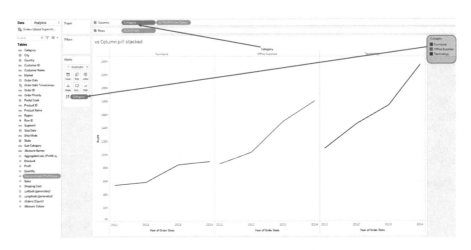

Figure 4-10. *Stacking dimensions in the Columns shelf*

Note   You can drop the same dimension in multiple shelves simultaneously (columns, rows, color, etc.) as highlighted in Figure 4-10.

CUSTOM COLOR PALETTES?

You can create your custom color palettes and save them in Tableau. I'm going to refer you to the almighty Google again but with the keyword Preferences. tps. Without going too much into details, it's an XML file (specifying the color hex codes of your custom palette) that you need to save in your Documents ➤ My Tableau Repository Folder.

4.3.2 Size Block

No surprises here. The Size block allows you to change the size of the visualizations. Let's build a quick visualization of a stacked bar chart of total profits generated by ship mode. You add the profit in the Rows column to sum them and drop Ship Mode in the Color block. This provides a single multicolor bar, as illustrated in the visualization on the left in Figure 4-11.

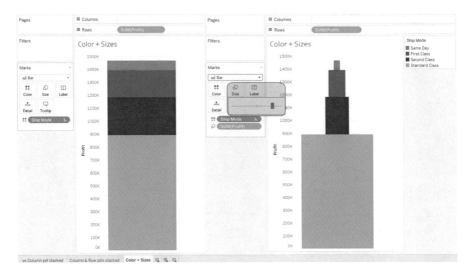

Figure 4-11. *Sizing up the graphs*

CHAPTER 4   THE CRUX OF TABLEAU

You can quickly see that the total profits are the highest in the standard shipping class and decrease as you move up to same-day shipping. But let's say you want to accentuate this and point out that total profits are very low on same-day shipping. Cmd/Ctrl+click **SUM(Profit)** in the Rows shelf and drop it into the Size block as well. This ensures that the total profits determine the width of the bars.

Homework   Show that ship mode does not influence the profitability of the orders. It might be tempting to conclude that same-day shipping mode is not profitable.

There is a drop-down tucked in sneakily above the Size, Color, and Label blocks. It is where you change the shapes of the visualizations. Now would be a good time as any to take a detour and check this out.

Let's make a small change to the visualization in Figure 4-12. Let's move the Profit pill from the Rows shelf to the Size block and simply shift the shape from a bar to a square in the drop-down. You have the beloved treemap. Fancy a packed bubble chart? Switch the square to a circle!

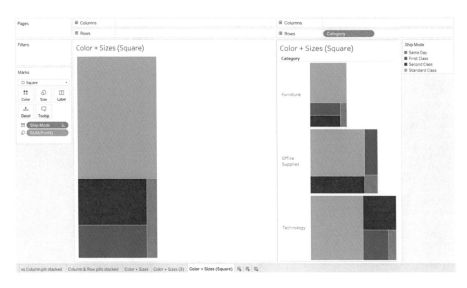

Figure 4-12. *Change the shapes*

4.3.3 Label Block

You're off to a great start with three blocks on the Marks card. You'll be able to craft about 90% of the typical graph types you need for your dashboard by playing with these combinations.

Let's run with the treemap to showcase the label functionality. As highlighted in Figure 4-13, drag Ship Mode onto the Label block. This allows you to label the visual elements in a chart. Clicking the Label block opens a pop-up that offers endless customization possibilities. For example, you can add custom text, changing the font, alignment, and so forth.

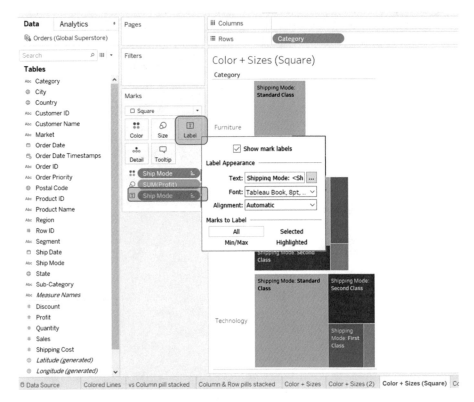

Figure 4-13. *Annotating with labels*

4.3.4 Detail Block

Let's go back to the basic bar chart to look at the Detail block closely. By now, you should be capable of building a bar chart with your eyes closed (almost!). You saw that adding a dimension to the label annotates the graph. In Figure 4-14, let's start with a simple "total sales by category" and add a segment to the Color block. Now there are three segments highlighted in each vertical bar. Let's then add Ship Mode to the Label block. Ship Mode is not part of the initial configuration of the visualization. So visually, nothing looks different apart from the added labels, which might initially seem randomly strewn about. As you hover your mouse over the bars, the bars are broken down into granular blocks. Each subblock represents the ship mode corresponding to the segment and category combination, and now the labels start to make more sense.

Figure 4-14. *Adding more details*

This is the same as adding Ship Mode to the Detail block instead. In essence, the Detail block breaks down a visual element into its granular details. There are three pills in the Marks section. The first pill segment dictates the color. The second and third pills are in ship mode, which provides the granular details within each segment.

Note There is a hierarchy in the order of the color and the details block. If you flip the segment and ship mode order, you get an adjacent visualization as in Figure 4-15.

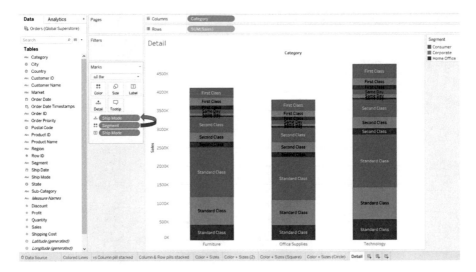

Figure 4-15. *Hierarchy in details*

4.3.5 Tooltip Block

You can continue to add more details into visualization, and there comes the point when the visualization becomes no longer meaningful or decipherable or a combination of both. Tooltips, fortunately, provide an elegant way to load more information without visually cramming your visualization. Used appropriately, tooltips can help you tell the right story effectively by reducing *chartjunk*.

> *The interior decoration of graphics generates a lot of ink that does not tell the viewer anything new. The purpose of decoration varies—to make the graphic appear more scientific and precise, to enliven the display, to give the designer an opportunity to exercise artistic skills. Regardless of its cause, it is all non-data-ink or redundant data-ink, and it is often chartjunk.*

> —Edward Tufte

Figure 4-16 shows the furniture segment ranks second in the number of sales across the three categories, but it ranks last in terms of percentage contribution toward profit. The triangle icon next to the sales and profit calculates the percentage contribution. This is discussed more in Chapter 6, which focuses on table calculations.

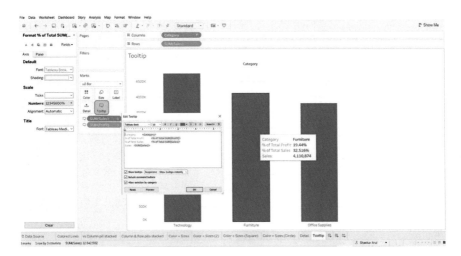

Figure 4-16. *Hierarchy in details*

Like the Label block, clicking the Tooltip block offers the opportunity to customize tooltip elements like font, alignment, and so on.

4.3.6 Angle and Path Blocks

The Angle and the Path blocks do not appear by default, and they appear when either the pie or the polygon shape is selected, respectively. You look at the Angle block in detail as you build the pie chart at the end of this chapter.

4.4 Filters

Figure 3-3 illustrated data sources filters and how they can help you filter the raw data upstream and get you exactly the data set you need for your analysis.

Sometimes, you'd like to filter your data conditionally for your analysis and not the entire data set. This is where the Filters pane comes into action. As shown in Figure 4-17, when you drag and drop country into the Filters pane, you are greeted with a pop-up box that provides a host of customization options. Let's keep it simple for now and start with the assumption that you're interested in Albania and Algeria for your analysis. You simply tick both the countries and click the **OK** button to confirm your filter selection.

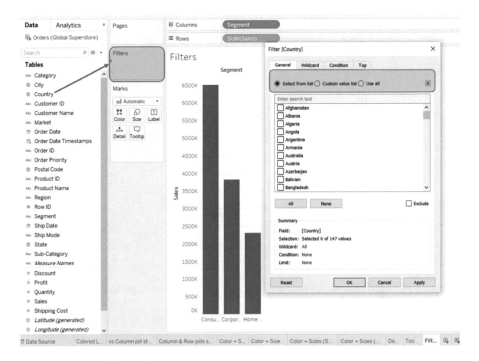

Figure 4-17. *Filter data*

You're now looking at data where the Country column contains either Albania or Algeria for this analysis. You can confirm this by right-clicking the Country pill in the Filters pane, as highlighted in Figure 4-18, and ticking the **Show Filter**. This option works well when you want to preselect a country by default for your filter. It can still change the filter values on the fly during your exploratory analysis or provide your end-users with the flexibility to change the filter values in dynamic dashboards (see Chapter 8).

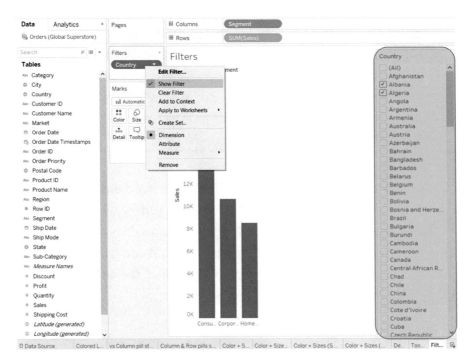

Figure 4-18. *Show the filter*

Look at the pop-up filter window in Figure 4-17. There are three options.

- **Select from list**
- **Custom value list**
- **Use all**

● SELECT FROM LIST VS. USE ALL?

There is a very subtle difference between the first and third options. The first option is used in Figure 4-18. It preselects certain values in a list. Let's imagine that you had four countries in your data set, and you had selected them all individually using the **Select from list** option in your filter.

Let's say there is a new value, Tuvalu, in the Country column when you refresh the data set. The filter is pre-ticked with only the four initial values you had chosen and did not select Tuvalu by default. If your initial thought was to pre-tick all the relevant values and not restrict it to the four, you might want to go with the **Use All** option instead. This way, your filter is preselected with all the relevant values in the column and not restricted to a few initial values. It all depends on what you try to achieve. You can go to bed and cover yourself or cover yourself and go to bed, so goes an adage in Tamil.

Figure 4-19 shows that the custom value list allows defining values that may or may not be in the initial list of values. Taking the example of Tuvalu, let's say you know that currently, the Country column does not contain this value, but in the future, you can predefine it and add it to your custom value list. This way, the filter is appropriately applied, the day when Tuvalu shows up in your country column.

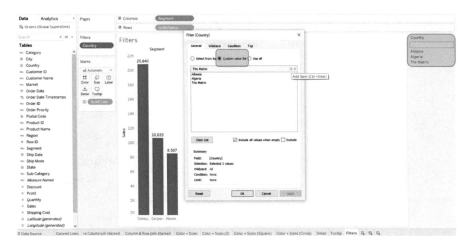

Figure 4-19. *Custom value list*

⚡ FILTERING ON THE FLY

You often want to filter and dive more deeply into certain outliers or interesting values as you conduct your exploratory analysis. In Tableau, it is as simple as right-clicking the value that you'd like to zoom into and then selecting **Keep only**. You can do this anywhere on a simple bar (see Figure 4-20(a)), a stacked bar (filtered on multiple values in Figure 4-20(b)), or individual values on a scatter plot (see Figure 4-20(c). You can click-and-drag a square over points of interest on a scatter plot before right-clicking.

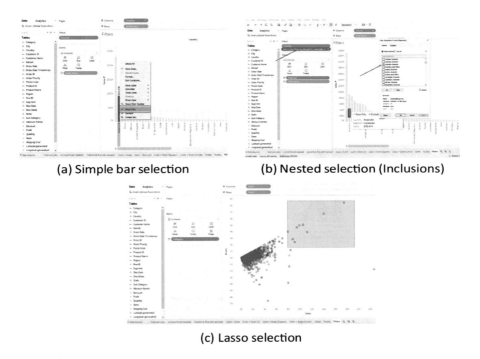

(a) Simple bar selection   (b) Nested selection (Inclusions)

(c) Lasso selection

Figure 4-20. *On-the-fly filtering*

4.5 Putting It All Together

Let's bring all the blocks together and build the "sneaky" pie chart shown in Figure 4-21. It's sneaky because building a humble pie chart is notoriously complicated in Tableau. The visualization you want to build displays the "Percentage contribution of profits by the market in each of the categories of products being sold." Start by dropping the category on the Columns shelf and selecting the **Pie** shape type in the Marks section. This creates three circles of uniform color under each of the categories. The Marks section is then populated with an extra block, Angle, which determines the size of the individual slices of the pie.

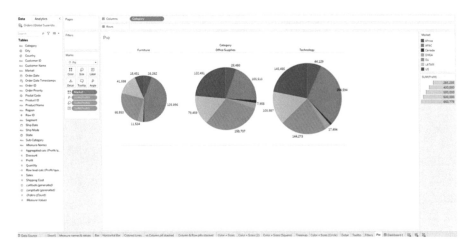

Figure 4-21. *The tricky pie*

The next step would be to drag the Market section onto the Color block. This creates six uniformly sized slices in each of the pie charts. You're starting to get closer to the end goal. Next, let's bring in the profits into the Angle block and the Size block. This ensures that the size of the slices and the entire pie are a function of the total profits.

4.6 Show Me

Knowing the four pillars of Tableau covered so far, you should be able to conjure up any visualization that you fancy. But sometimes, when you lack inspiration, you could always turn to the Show Me ribbon. Sometimes they can help speed up the construction of your visualization; that is, building a simple menial table with two measures in Tableau can be time-consuming, and that's where the **Show Me** button could come to the rescue. In Figure 4-22, clicking the Show Me button unveils a pop-up window with a host of visualizations (some active and some grayed-out based on the values in the Rows and Columns shelves).

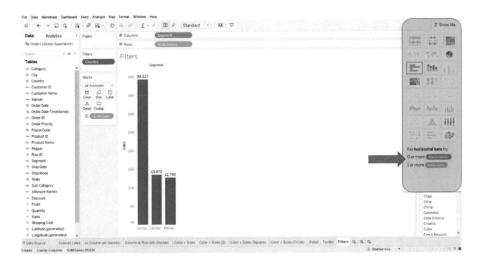

Figure 4-22. *The "Show me" magic*

Hovering over a visualization provides a minimum required list of dimensions and measures.

4.7 Sheets, Dashboards and Stories

So far, you have created a new sheet for every visualization built. When you want to bring all the analyses together and start your data storytelling, you have two options: dashboards and stories (see Figure 4-23).

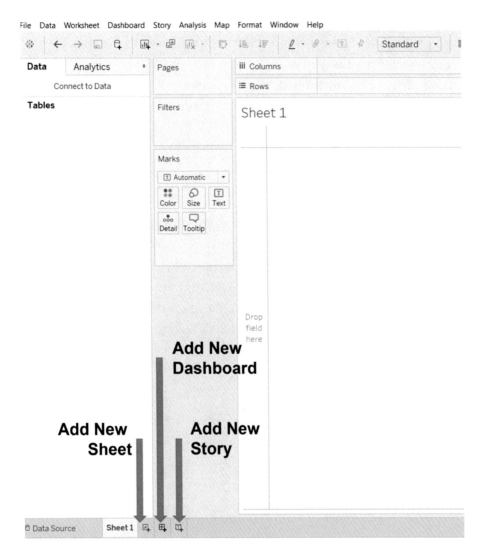

Figure 4-23. *Sheets, dashboards, and stories*

A *dashboard* brings together the various analysis sheets in a single sheet. You can then apply global filters in your dashboard across all the sheets or use values in certain visualizations to cross-filter other visualizations in your dashboard. Building a dashboard is an art.

If you cram together too many analyses, over time, the dashboard becomes illegible. You learn more about dashboards in Chapter 8.

Stories are a relatively new addition to Tableau. A *story* helps you build a strong narrative by stitching together various sheets. A story allows you to add more context and highlight certain insights and salient points in your analysis.

4.8 Summary

This chapter discussed Tableau's building blocks, which help build and customize your visualizations. Combining these blocks in creative ways provides the opportunity to build more advanced visualizations. The next chapter dives into the calculations and explains how to prepare custom-calculated columns for visualizations. You also see how to combine and merge disparate data sources using Tableau's blending and modeling capacities.

CHAPTER 5

Calculations

Most often, data needs preparation and manipulation. For example, you might have to calculate new KPIs, look up values from another table, scale up or down certain columns of values, or calculate percentages. Tableau provides the tools required to automate these time-consuming steps. You have the option either to prepare the data upstream in a tool such as Tableau Prep or Alteryx or directly within Tableau. This book covers the possibilities within Tableau. Let's start with one of the simplest tasks in which business users often are faced with grouping values.

✐TASK: GROUP A LIST OF COUNTRIES INTO VARIOUS REGIONS

You could easily resolve this task in Excel with a VLOOKUP by creating a lookup table (shown in Table 5-1) and using the VLOOKUP formula in a new column to look up the appropriate regions in the list of countries.

Table 5-1. *Lookup Value to Create Grouping*

Country	Regional Mapping
Mexico	North America
US	North America
Canada	North America
France	Western Europe
Italy	Southern Europe

© Shankar Arul 2022
S. Arul, *Tableau for Business Users*, https://doi.org/10.1007/978-1-4842-7786-7_5

You could achieve the same result in Tableau in three different ways.

- Using the Group functionality to do grouping

- Data blending with relationships (section 5.3.1)

- Joins (section 5.3.2)

Let's start with the easiest approach using grouping. Right-click the column (country) that you want to group, and then click **Create ➤ Group**, where you can custom group the values manually as in Figure 5-1.

Every time the data is refreshed, Tableau automatically creates this new column with this mapping. The caveat with this method is that it works well for a handful of values (less than 10). As your mapping tends to grow, it's much easier to handle this with relationships or joins, as discussed in section 5.3. The last two methods help you industrialize this mapping to bigger data sets.

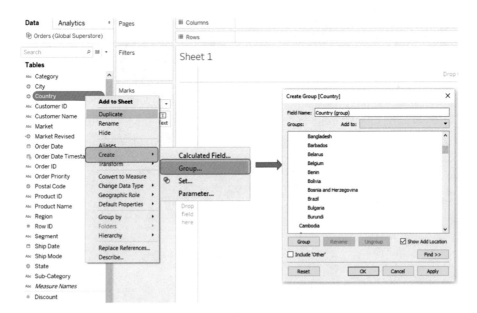

Figure 5-1. *Grouping values with aliases*

You might want to do the same grouping but with numeric quantities. In the superstore data set, there is a **Quantity** column that contains the values 1–14. Let's say you were conducting a study on how quantities were affecting your bottom-line profitability. When you ship less than five items, your shipping costs are low, and therefore, you generate higher profit margins. But on the other hand, the profit margins drop slightly with every incremental item but remain consistent till ten items before the next steep drop occurs. To visually represent this, you want to group the quantities into three buckets based on the magnitude (1-5, 6–10, and >10).

As illustrated in Figure 5-2, right-click the **Quantity** column, and under the Create submenu, click **Group**. This opens the window on the right to select multiple values. Click **Group** to create your desired grouping.

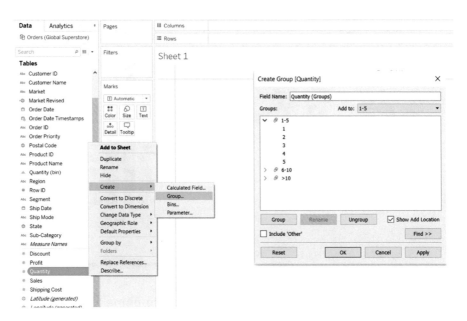

Figure 5-2. *Grouping numerical values*

✈ HISTOGRAMS TO UNDERSTAND THE DISTRIBUTION OF NUMERIC COLUMNS?

Let's say during your exploratory data analysis, you want to construct a histogram to understand the distribution of numeric quantities. Instead of selecting a group, if you chose Bins, Tableau automatically creates equal-sized bins. In the Quantity column, Tableau suggests a bin size of 1.77 (probably using the Freedman-Diaconis rule). It's then as easy as dragging Quantity (bin) into the Shelf column to get a count of the quantity in the Rows shelf, which provides a frequency distribution of the values in the Quantity column.

Figure 5-3. *Histograms in Tableau*

One other frequent data preparation step is to combine two columns. For example, imagine two columns with first name and last name, respectively. You would need to concatenate them into one column. In Excel, the & operator rescues in a formula (=A2 &", "&B2).

Figure 5-4 shows how to combine the Segment and Ship Mode columns. Start by clicking the **Segment** and **Ship Mode** dimensions while pressing the Ctrl/Cmd keys and selecting **Create ➤ Combined Field**. This creates a new combined column, which you can then right-click and select **Edit combined column** to specify the delimiter between the values of the column.

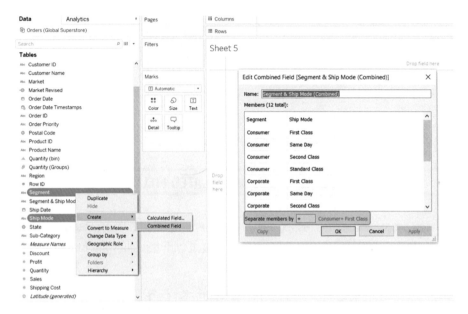

Figure 5-4. *Concatenating columns*

5.1 Calculated Fields

Calculated fields allow you to apply formulas to modify existing data columns or combine multiple fields. The superstore data set has a Shipping Cost column and a Quantity column. You want to compute the unit shipping cost by dividing the Shipping Cost column by the Quantity column. Start by right-clicking **Shipping Cost** and selecting **Create ➤ Calculated Field**. This opens a pop-up window, as shown in Figure 5-5. Now using basic mathematical operators, you can string together formulas to your heart's content.

Figure 5-5. *Calculated columns*

☞ NULL TRAPS IN CALCULATED FIELDS?

Watch out for null values, especially in your numeric columns. For example, replace the null profits in the Consumer segment with the following formula in a new column called Null'd profit.

IF [Segment]="Consumer" THEN NULL ELSE [Profit] END

Figure 5-6 shows that you need to be careful when adding columns with null values. The ZN function could come in handy in such cases to replaces the nulls with zeros.

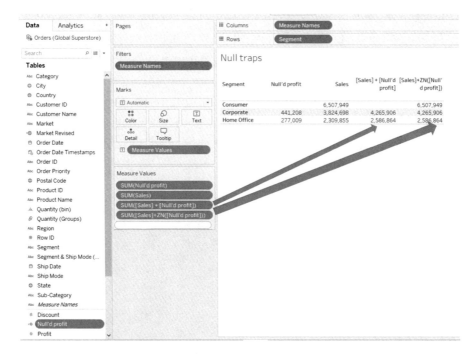

Figure 5-6. *Null values need to be replaced with zeros before calculations*

Clicking the arrow on the icon in the right in the pop-up window reveals all the various functions available in Tableau. Tableau's documentation provides an extensive list of Tableau functions at your disposal.

5.2 Row Level, Aggregation, and Disaggregation

When you author formulas in Tableau, by referencing the column names directly, the calculations are done at the level of each row. For example, **[Profit]**/**[Quantity]** calculates the value of this column for each row by dividing the respective values of profit and sales at each row. Hence called *row-level operations*. On the other hand, if you were to modify the formula slightly to **SUM([Profit]) / SUM([Quantity])**, these values are aggregated to the appropriate level of detail visible in your visualization before the division occurs. For example, your row shelf contains the Segment column, as illustrated in Figure 5-7. Then the ratios would be calculated for each of the three unique values (consumer, corporate, and home office) by aggregating profits and quantity before dividing.

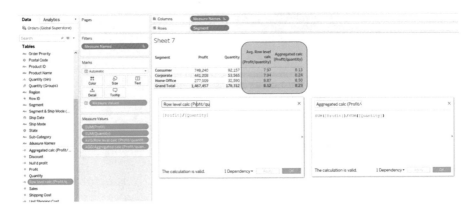

Figure 5-7. *Average of Averages is not the same as consolidated averages*

By default, Tableau aggregate the measures for you. On the menu bar, **Analysis ➤ Aggregate Measures** is ticked by default. If you do not want Tableau to aggregate the measures and show the row-level data, toggling this tick mark gets the results you want. (You can achieve the same result by converting the measure into a dimension.) This option is useful, especially while you're building scatter plots where you want to compare two measures against each other at a row level but not aggregated.

5.3 Bringing in More Data

For fast and reactive Tableau dashboards and reports, it's a good idea to have a data source in which you have already consolidated your data at the right level of aggregation. But most often, this is a dream in a utopian world, and you're often confronted with various data sources (databases, stray Excel and CSV files, etc.). Luckily, Tableau provides various options to consolidate your disparate data sources. The logic is the same after you import the data, and it's the import steps that vary between the various data sources. The first two in the following list are essentially the same. Let's look at the process of importing another tab in the sheet.

- Another tab in the Excel sheet (the same as importing another Excel file)

- Import a CSV file

- MySQL Database—SQL

5.3.1 From Excel/CSV

The examples covered so far used the orders sheet from the Global Superstore .xlsx file. Unfortunately, this data set does not contain the sales representatives responsible for the various geographic regions. Let's say you want to compare the performance of the various sales representatives relative to each other and eventually evaluate their performance over the past few years. In a world of Excel, now would be the time for a VLOOKUP to shine in all its glory.

To do the same in Tableau, let's import data from the People tab. It contains the sales representatives responsible for the different geographic regions and blends it with the orders data. You can click the New Data Source button (highlighted in Figure 5-8). Or, on the menu ribbon, you could select **Data ➤ New Data Source**. Or, you could navigate to the **Data Source** tab and click the **Add** button. All roads lead to Rome!

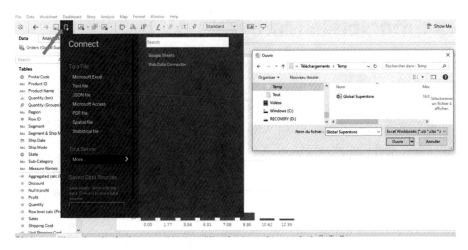

Figure 5-8. *Bring in some data from another tab*

Once you have imported the data from the People tab, two data sources are listed under the Data pane at the top, and you can confirm that by navigating to the Data menu. Clicking **Edit Blend Relationships** opens the pop-up shown in Figure 5-9.

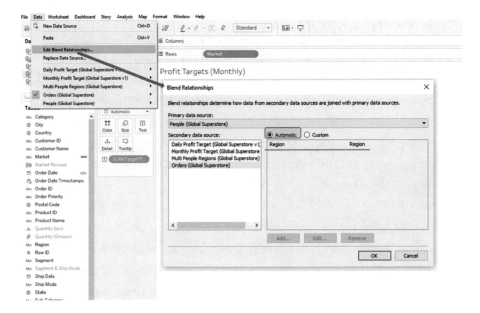

Figure 5-9. *Data blending*

Had you peeked at the People tab while you imported the data, you would have seen that it contains two columns: Person and Region. Tableau automatically recognizes that there is a Region column in the orders tab and automatically defines a relationship.

Note   The column names must be the same in the data sources for automatic detection to work.

If Tableau incorrectly defines the relationships automatically or if you need to add or edit the relationship, the **Add** and **Edit** buttons open a pop-up similar to what's shown in Figure 5-10. It allows you to select the right column on either side (primary and secondary data).

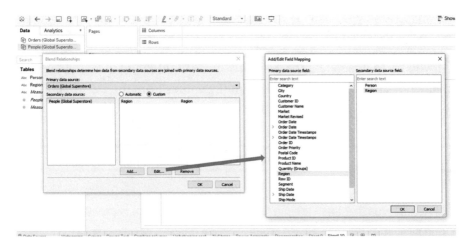

Figure 5-10. *Adding/editing the blending relationship*

Now that the data sources have been added, and the relationships between the tables have been defined, you are all set for data blending. First, let's bring the Region field into the rows in the Orders table and then switch to the People table. Note the small link highlighted in red as step 3a

61

in Figure 5-11. When highlighted, this link ensures that the relationship is active, and now when you bring in the Person field, you get the name of the sales representative assigned to each region.

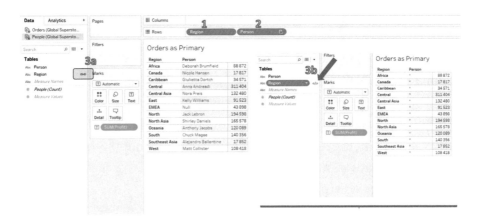

Figure 5-11. *Data blending*

If you try to deactivate the relationship as highlighted in step 3b, Tableau does not know how to bring in the values from the Person field in the current view and instead shows an asterisk.

✈ ATTR

ATTR indicates that there are multiple values, while Tableau is expecting a single value. In the Person field in the example, there is exactly one sales representative per region, and hence Tableau had no issue displaying it. On the other hand, if you have multiple sales representatives assigned to each region, Tableau displays a * next to the region, indicating multiple values. One workaround makes the relationship 1:1 by adding more granular details to the People tab to ensure that the relationship between the two tabs is unique or, even better, try leveraging *relationships* (see section 5.5).

Whenever you blend data in Tableau, you can identify the primary and secondary data sources in your blend by the blue and red tick marks next to the data sources, respectively (highlighted in Figure 5-12). Double-clicking the Region pill shows that Tableau applies ATTR by default to ensure that one value is brought to the front.

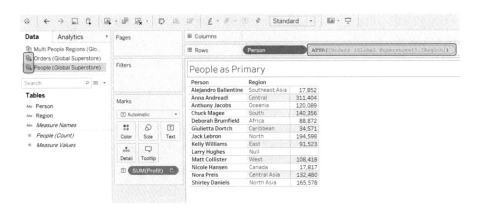

Figure 5-12. *Data blending*

A subtle point to keep in mind on your blending extravaganza by default, the unique values in your primary data source constitute the starting point which is then completed with relevant information from your secondary data sources. There are 13 unique regions and 13 unique sales representatives in the data set. As a result, you could start with the orders data as the primary and people as the secondary or vice-versa, and you're sure to have 13 lines in either visualization. But let's say there are six sales representatives in the People tab. In that case, the order of the primary and secondary data sources matter. I'll let you think about why that happens.

This process of dynamically defining relationships after the data has been imported is essentially called *data blending*. You could achieve the same result through joins as well, which is slightly upstream in the process of importing. As you import the data, you directly specify the relationships (left, right, outer, or inner join) among the various data sources and import the data into Tableau.

For a more detailed explanation of joins and how they are different from relationships, please refer to Tableau's help pages at `https://help.tableau.com/v2020.2/public/desktop/en-us/datasource_relationships_learnmorepage.htm`.

Do keep in mind that with blending, the relationships between the data sources are defined dynamically. As a result, the data sources are not physically joined and materialized as a table. But on the other hand, with joins, the relationship is concretely manifested by creating a flat table (denormalized) containing the columns from the various data sources. Tableau recommends avoiding the use of joins as much as possible and using either relationship or blending capabilities.

In the Data Source tab, you first need to double-click the Orders brick or the Open option before joining the secondary data source. Now when you drop in your secondary data source, Tableau shows a Venn diagram that allows you to specify the join type, as highlighted in Figure 5-13.

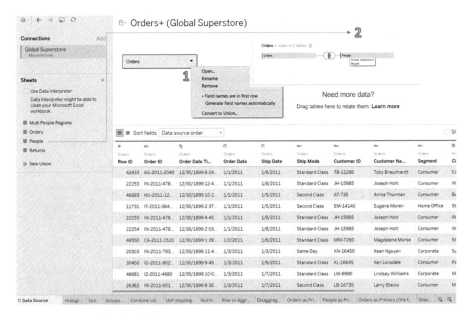

Figure 5-13. *Data joins*

Again, essentially there are four types of joins: left, right, inner, and outer. YouTube has a plethora of informational videos for those who wish to dig deeper on the topic of joins.

5.3.2 From MySQL

So far, you have worked with data imported from Excel and CSV. Let's look at the process of importing data from a database such as MySQL. The process is the same for all similar databases. As highlighted in step 1 in Figure 5-14, you need to fill in the credentials of the database you're trying to connect to. In this example, I have connected to a MySQL database running locally on my computer at IP address 127.0.0.1 (localhost) and default port 3306. You need to provide the database name and the username and password to complete the connection.

Figure 5-14. *New Custom SQL*

Once connected, Tableau shows the various tables available in your database. You can either directly drag and drop the tables or use **New Custom SQL** to more precisely pull in the columns at the granularity you need.

The following is a small SQL query to give you a sample of how this works.

```
SELECT
a.market,

b.new_market as revised_market,
a.order_date,

SUM(a.profit)
FROM

orders AS a

LEFT JOIN market_groupings AS b
ON a.market = b.market
```

The query pulls in the market, order date, and total profits from the table orders and merges it with the Market Groupings table to get the revised market groupings. The result of this SQL query is a table with four columns that you can use as a data source in your visualizations. Whenever you combine two or more data sources, the level of granularity (cardinality) is extremely important. To illustrate this, let's look at the typical budgeting exercise that business analysts and financial controllers undertake on a quarterly, monthly, or even daily.

5.4 The Importance of Cardinality: A Practical Example

Imagine the financial team has defined forecast targets for profits of the seven different markets by month. Now when you want to compare the actual performance of the profits in the Orders table against the forecast targets, you cannot do it directly as the level of granularity is not the same. The Orders table is much more granular as it contains individual orders by market, country, product, and order ID, while the targets are defined at the level of market and month.

To consolidate the two tables, you need to ensure that they have the same level of granularity on either side. Let's say the finance team also has the targets defined for the seven markets by day. It is a little more straightforward as the dates are at the same level of granularity on either side. Let's define the blending relationships for the Orders table and the two target tables (daily and monthly), respectively.

Once you import the Daily Profit Target and Monthly Profit Target tabs from the Global Superstore v1.xlsx file, follow the steps (see section 5.3.1) to define the blending relationship between the orders and targets table. For the daily targets table, choose **Market** and **MDY**(date) on either of the tables. (MDY stands for month-day-year in Tableau). Since the targets are defined monthly in the monthly targets data, be sure to choose the market and MY (month-year) on the date on either side, as highlighted in Figure 5-15.

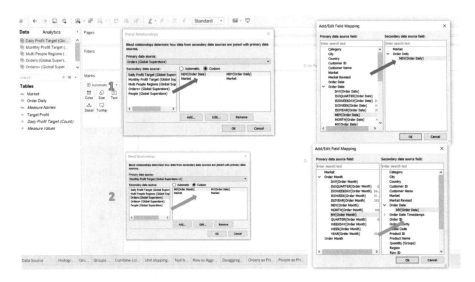

Figure 5-15. *Blending relationships at different levels of granularity*

Let's do a quick sanity check on the targets in the two data sources. The sum of target profits in either data source is $3,514,968. Let's start building a comparison of targets against actual profit. You could take two approaches depending on the data source (primary) that you start with. In the first approach, let's use the monthly profit target as the starting point (primary data source). Drag the market and target profits from the monthly profit target data source onto the visualization pane. Bring in the actual profits from the Orders table in the second step. The Orders table gets a small red tick indicating that it's a secondary data source. Let's activate the blending relationship on the market and order date. You get the same total target profits of $3.5 million, as expected.

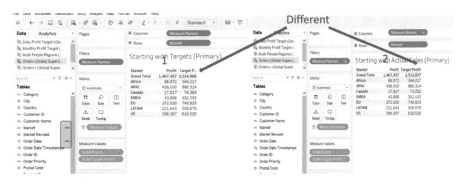

Figure 5-16. *Blending at market and order date*

Now for the second approach, let's start with the orders as the primary data source (blue tick) and complete it with the monthly targets data. Let's activate the blending relationship on the market and the order month on the target data source. Surprisingly, the total target profits don't match the total of $3,514,968, but instead, you get a total target profit of $3,513,837. You're missing $1,131.

This head-scratcher is primarily related to the activation of blending relationships. Let me give you the solution before explaining the why and how behind the fix. Keep the market relationship activated while deactivating the order month to get the true total target profits on either side, as highlighted in Figure 5-17.

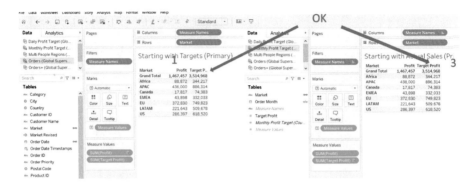

Figure 5-17. *Blending at the market level*

Let's now try to explain this mysterious phenomenon. If you look at the target table, it is exhaustive in terms of targets defined by the market and by month (i.e., every month from January 2011 to December 2014 has a target assigned by market). But on the contrary, there was not a sale every month in each of the markets. As a result, the second approach (see Figure 5-16) brought in the months when a sale was made as the Orders table was the primary data source. You blended this against the target profits at the regional and monthly levels. Hence Tableau did not bring in the targets for those "market and month combinations" where no sales were made.

Removing the blend on the month and keeping it on the market tells Tableau to bring in all sales at the market level and compare it against the total target profits irrespective of the month. This fixes the issue in Figure 5-17. Figure 5-18 shows that Canada did not generate any profits in January 2012 while it had a target of $1,131, which was the missing amount. I let you conduct the same operation on the daily targets table to identify markets and days when no sales occurred.

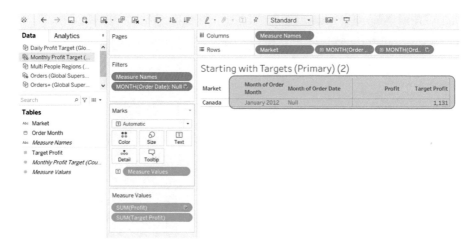

Figure 5-18. *The discrepancy comes from Canada not making a sale*

⚡ BLENDS ARE EQUIVALENT TO LEFT JOINS

The one key takeaway from this lengthy exercise on cardinality is to keep in mind that blends are equivalent to left joins. You start with the rows on your primary data source and how you activate the blending relationship. You might bring in or exclude rows from the secondary data source.

5.5 Data Modeling

Now that you've got a firm grasp on data blending in Tableau and the nitty-gritty details about the order of joins, you might be wondering, "Couldn't Tableau make this easier?" You are not alone, as Tableau seems to have taken notice. In version 2020.2, Tableau introduced *data modeling* and *relationships*, which work similarly to what is seen in competing tools like Power BI. The data model enables you to define relationships between various data sources. Tableau does the heavy lifting behind the screens to pull in the right data at the right level of cardinality. Let's walk through the previous example of target vs. actual comparisons achieved through blending but this time with the aid of data modeling and relationships.

Let's go to the Data Source tab and drag in the Orders and the Daily Profit Target tables. As soon as you drag in the Targets table (highlighted in 1), you see an orange line (informally as the *noodle*) and a pop-up window that show the relationship (highlighted in 2). In this case, let's select Market and Order Date/Order Daily on either side, respectively, and close the relationships panel as shown in Figure 5-19.

Figure 5-19. *Data modeling step 1 noodle*

When you navigate back to the sheets, Tableau shows all the data sources for which a relationship is designed. With blends, you had to pay attention to where you started; otherwise, the numbers did not exactly match expectations.

With relationships, the totals are the same in either case, irrespective of your starting point (i.e., markets from the Orders table or the daily target table).

Tableau added an extra row on the second table, as shown in Figure 5-20, where you start with the markets from the Orders table. Tableau shows that there are markets with defined daily targets which have not made a corresponding sale.

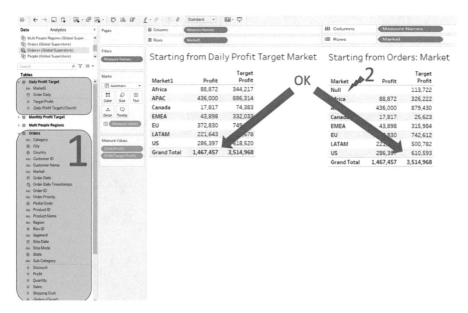

Figure 5-20. *Data modeling step 2*

✈ LOGICAL VS. PHYSICAL LAYER?

Remember that whenever you see a noodle (link), you're in the logical layer (the results are not manifested as flat tables). On the other hand, whenever you see a Venn diagram, you're in the physical layer where joins are made and flat denormalized tables are created.

A handy recap of Relationships vs. Joins vs. Blends is presented below in Figure 5-21 and more information is available at this link: `https://help.tableau.com/v2021.4/pro/desktop/en-us/relate_tables.htm#Relationhttps://help.tableau.com/v2021.4/pro/desktop/en-us/relate_tables.htm`

RELATIONSHIPS	JOINS
Defined between logical tables in the Relationship canvas (logical layer)	Defined between physical tables in the Join/Union canvas (physical layer)
Don't require you to define a join type	Require join planning and join type
Act like containers for tables that are joined or unioned	Are merged into their logical table
Only data relevant to the viz is queried. Cardinality and referential integrity settings can be adjusted to optimize queries.	Run as part of every query
Level of detail is at the aggregate for the viz	Level of detail is at the row level for the single table
Join types are automatically formed by Tableau based on the context of analysis. Tableau determines the necessary joins based on the measures and dimensions in the viz.	Join types are static and fixed in the data source, regardless of analytical context. Joins and unions are established prior to analysis and don't change.
Rows are not duplicated	Merged table data can result in duplication
Unmatched records are included in aggregates, unless explicitly excluded	Unmatched records are omitted from the merged data
Create independent domains at multiple levels of detail.	Support scenarios that require a single table of data, such as extract filters, row level security, aggregation

RELATIONSHIPS	BLENDS
Defined in the data source	Defined in the worksheet between a primary and a secondary data source
Can be published	Can't be published
All tables are equal semantically	Depend on selection of primary and secondary data sources, and how those data sources are structured.
Support full outer joins	Only support left joins
Computed locally	Computed as part of the SQL query
Related fields are fixed	Related fields vary by sheet (can be customized on a sheet-by-sheet basis)

Figure 5-21. *Relationships vs. joins vs. blend*

5.6 Summary

In this chapter, you saw how to create calculated columns, as you would do in Excel, to build the visualizations and analysis. You also saw how to bring in more than one data source and tie them all together with the functionalities of blending and modeling. In the next chapter, you take a deeper look at table calculations that replicate Excel tables and express advanced comparisons and ratios.

CHAPTER 6

Tables and Table Calculations

Unfortunately, Tableau sometimes tends to make the easiest of things unbelievably hard. For example, let's say you build a simple bar chart to show the profits by market, as highlighted in Figure 6-1, and want to change it to a table.

Figure 6-1. *Show Me faster*

Armed with what you know so far, you would get five extra points if you switch the chart type from bar to text. But unfortunately, that would not get you the result you had in mind and is one of the most frequent points of

© Shankar Arul 2022
S. Arul, *Tableau for Business Users*, https://doi.org/10.1007/978-1-4842-7786-7_6

frustration for beginners. Unfortunately, the only way to do this manually is to fastidiously rearrange the pills (market in rows and SUM(Profit) on the text card in the Marks section. This is where the Show Me pane can come in handy. In a click, you would be able to flip to a table or even the infamous pie chart.

⚡ ADDING MEASURES TO TABLES

Now let's say you managed to put together a simple table with your profits by market and you want to add the total sales and a column. You need to be careful to drag the sales pill on top of the existing Profit column, as highlighted on the right in Figure 6-2. Tableau creates two rows if you drop them on the text shelf (as highlighted on the left). This is not what you had in mind. You could still click Table on the Show Me ribbon to force Tableau to create two columns.

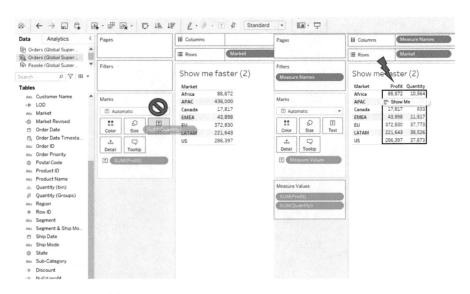

Figure 6-2. *Table tips*

The Show Me table can only take you so far. Let's get our hands dirty and build a table from scratch to understand the nitty-gritty details. Let's answer some questions based on the table in Figure 6-3. What are the profit and sales by region? Break it down by the number of items you're selling. Is there any correlation between sales and profits? Are there any outliers in terms of regions? I admit that you could build better visualizations to answer these questions, but let's stick to this table for pedagogical reasons.

Market ⇕ ▾		Quantity (Groups)		
		1-5	6-10	>10
Africa	Profit	61,765	23,800	3,306
	Sales	555,699	192,572	35,503
APAC	Profit	268,528	153,482	13,990
	Sales	2,222,196	1,235,901	127,647
Canada	Profit	12,015	5,481	321
	Sales	48,934	15,915	2,079
EMEA	Profit	37,735	6,855	-692
	Sales	549,226	214,409	42,526
EU	Profit	242,880	118,498	11,452
	Sales	1,875,659	945,902	116,529
LATAM	Profit	138,144	75,948	7,552
	Sales	1,430,273	674,387	59,945
US	Profit	196,644	75,201	14,551
	Sales	1,503,737	717,353	76,111

Figure 6-3. *Table from scratch*

You can effectively build this table in four steps, as illustrated in Figure 6-4.

1. Drag the market and the quantity (groups) that you created in Chapter 5 into the row and column shelves.

   - Profits and sales must be two rows next to each market. Here comes the tricky part. You need to drag **Measure Names** next to the market. The rows are populated with **No Measure Value**.

2. Drag **Measure Values** onto the **Text** shelf, which creates a row for every measure.

3. Tableau handily adds the measure names in the Filter pane, which filters the unwanted measures and keeps the profit and sales that you need.

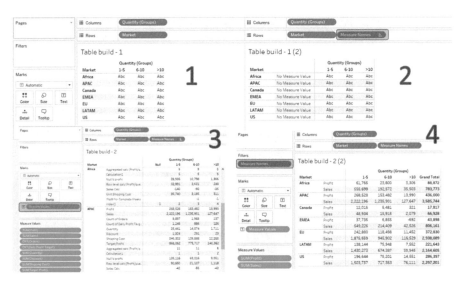

Figure 6-4. *Table from scratch in four steps*

If you need to add a new dynamic row that gives the total profit by sales for each market and quantity group intersection, you can double-click the **Measure Values** pane and enter the **SUM([Profit])/ SUM([Sales])** formula to add a new row.

6.1 Table Totals

Once you've got a pretty table, the next logical step would be to add grand totals along the rows or columns. Switch to the **Analysis** tab (highlighted in Figure 6-5), and as you drag the totals onto the visualization pane, you can then choose the Totals type. Or else, you could achieve the same result from the Analysis drop-down on the menu bar. The **Totals** options provide more customization options, such as displaying the columns' grand total at the top or bottom of the table, adding subtotals, and so forth. You can also decide to aggregate the numbers as average, minimum, or maximum in the Totals field.

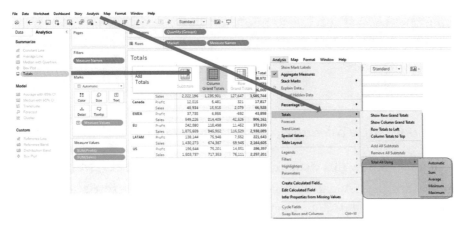

Figure 6-5. *Table totals*

6.2 Table Calculations

Table calculations help you narrow down on answers to advanced analytic questions. For example, suppose you want to visualize the evolution of the percentage split of sales across the three segments in all the markets over the last four years. It's a lot easier to start with a table to ensure that the numbers make sense before flipping to a pretty chart which might seem a little counterintuitive at first.

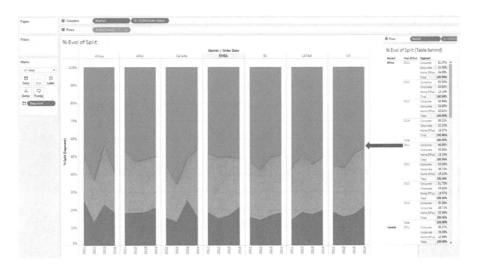

Figure 6-6. *Table calculations lay the foundation*

Before building this visualization, let's start nice and easy with a few simple warm-up Tableau calculations. For the following exercises, let's stick to *running totals* since the logic remains the same across the various table calculation functions.

6.2.1 Table and Pane Down and Across

Let's say you're doing a deep dive into the year 2011 and want to see how the profits have been growing cumulatively over the months in the year. The illustration in Figure 6-7 helps answer the question. The first two examples in this section 6.2.1 concerning a simple table.

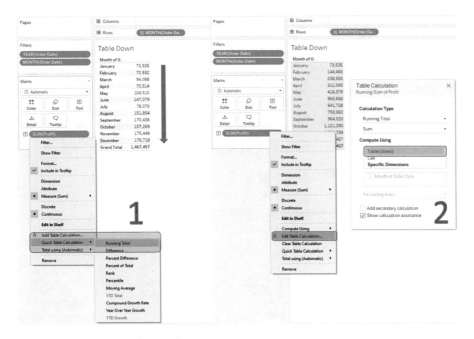

Figure 6-7. *Table (down)*

The **Quick Table Calculation** menu is helpful. Once you have selected **Running Total**, right-click and choose **Edit Table Calculation** to see what Tableau is doing behind the scenes. It is running a simple Table (down) calculation. If the months are along the columns instead of the rows, the table calculations become Table (across) instead of a Table (down), as shown in Figure 6-8.

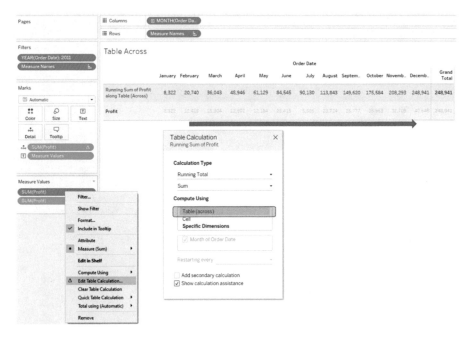

Figure 6-8. *Table (across)*

The table is the container or holder which contains the rows and columns of data. As you add more dimensions to a table, the table then gets further broken down into panes.

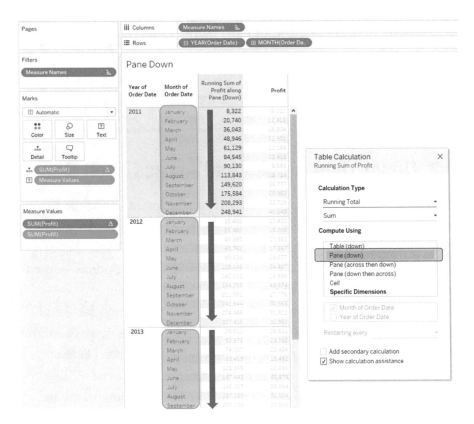

Figure 6-9. *Pane (down)*

When you add a table calculation, Tableau applies a Table (down) or Table (across) calculation through your entire table. For example, let's say you want to analyze the cumulative performance by month, not only for one year but across the years. Let's remove the filter and add the year dimension ahead of the month dimension. In this example, your table is broken into four panes because there are four years of data. **Edit Table Calculation** now reveals an extra option, which is **Pane (down)**. The running total resets at the end of each pane, giving the right cumulative total of each year. Switching the year and month from the row to the column shelf makes it a Pane (across) calculation.

⚡ WHERE DO CALCULATIONS RESET IN TABLE CALCULATIONS?

When you click Edit Table Calculations, Tableau highlights the scope of your table or pane calculations. It resets to zero at the end of the highlighted zone and restarts the calculations in the new pane.

6.2.2 Down Then Across and Across Then Down

Let's kick it up a notch, add an extra dimension (segment) along the columns, and focus on quarterly profits instead of monthly profits to simplify the table. Now that there is a pane across the rows (years) and segments along the columns, Tableau presents a few extra options—**down then across** and **across then down**—for both Table and Pane.

In Figure 6-10, you illustrate the **down then across** for both Table and Pane. In the **Table (down then across)** option, Tableau goes down the entire list of rows with the running total for the first segment and then climbs back to the next segment to continue the running total. In the Edit Table Calculation window under Specific Dimensions, all three dimensions are selected. In **Pane (down then across)**, the yellow zone stops at the end of 2011, indicating that the running total resets at the end of every year. Under **Specific Dimensions**, the year is unticked, whereas the segment and quarter are both ticked.

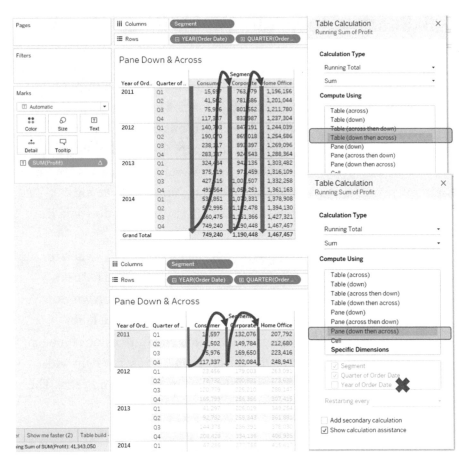

Figure 6-10. *Down and Across*

In **across then down**, the order of operation is transposed. The running total goes horizontally to the end of the list before continuing from the beginning of the subsequent rows.

6.2.3 Shortcut to Reading Table Calculations in English

Both **across then down** and **down then across** can help you through small tables with a maximum of three dimensions to visualize the flow of the calculations. But, as you add more dimensions or need finer granular control over the calculations, it's better to master the Specific Dimensions section in the **Edit Table Calculation** window. At first glance, it's not the most intuitive menu, and most analysts don't even know that you can reorder the rows in the Specific Dimensions list by holding down on the values.

Instead of relying on Down and Across calculations, let's switch to Specific Dimensions directly, as highlighted in Figure 6-11. There is a method to the madness in reading the **Edit Table Calculation** window while using **Specific Dimensions**, which helps you crush the table calculations once and for all. Start with the unticked dimensions for each segment, follow with calculating the running total, and wrap it up with the ticked dimensions in the reverse order (i.e., by quarter and year). The following is a formula for this.

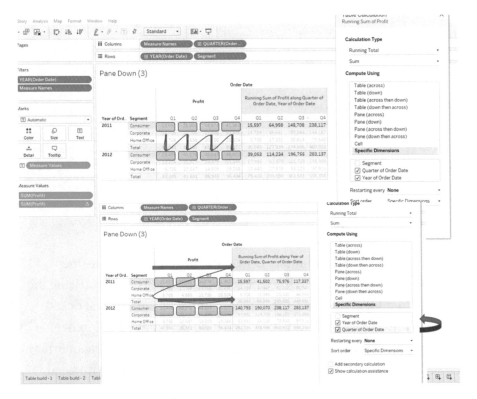

Figure 6-11. *Down and across*

(For each segment, calculate the running total by quarter and year.)

Full credit of this amazing formulation goes to Andy Kriebel and his amazing blog post at www.vizwiz.com/2017/02/table-calcs.html.

Figure 6-12. *Reading table calculations in English*

Let's look at another example. Let's say you want to compute the cumulative profits for each of the categories across the quarters. Using the same methodology, you leave the category unticked and the rest ticked. (The years can be ticked or unticked, and it doesn't make a difference, do you see why?) But now, when the calculation flows to end the quarter for a segment and restarts at the consecutive segment for Q1, you need to reset the totals as it doesn't make sense. The **Restarting every** option conveniently allows you to reset the totals for each segment.

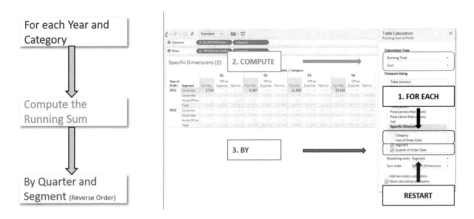

Figure 6-13. *Reading Table calculations in English example 2*

6.2.4 Formulation of Table Calculations

In section 3.4, you saw how to rephrase questions analytically. In case you forgot, let me jog your memory with this illustration.

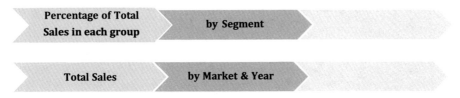

Let's start by listing the measure that you're trying to aggregate and follow it up with the dimension to break it down and apply the filtering conditions. As you might recall, you can stack the questions on top of each other as they grow in complexity.

Let's take the example question that drove the visualization in Figure 6-6: "Evolution of the percentage split of sales across the three segments in all the markets over the last four years." You can slice by dimensions in the reverse order. So, in this case, you could visualize the question and then switch the sales to the percentage of total instead of absolute numbers.

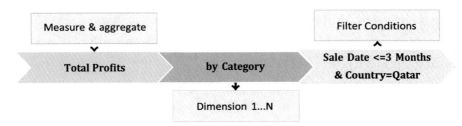

Also make sure to switch the calculations to **Pane (down)** from Table (down), which is the default. Once the table is in place, it's easy to flip it into an area chart using the Show Me wizard. Whenever you see Percentage of, Running Total, Differences, Moving Average, Year on Year, and so forth, always think table calculations.

6.2.5 Comparing YoY, WoW, and MoM

Let's use these amazing table calculations. Year over year, month over month, and all variants of these comparisons lend themselves perfectly well to table calculations.

Figure 6-14. *YoY calculations pitfalls and workarounds*

As illustrated in step 1, let's start with a simple use case by dropping in the year (order date). Now, using table calculations, you can easily calculate the percentage difference between the years. For some diabolical reason, let's say you decide to exclude 2012 from the analysis. In step 2, 2012 is filtered out, but unfortunately, Tableau now calculates the percentage difference of 2013 over the year 2011 instead of 2012 as it's the value in the previous row. A quick fix for this is to use the **Show Missing Values** option if the dimension using for the percentage difference calculation is continuous. (In this case, it's the year, which is a continuous date variable.)

Let's take it a step further and try to do Year over year comparisons by country as illustrated in Figure 6-15. Armenia and Nepal did not have any sales in 2011, 2012, and 2014, respectively. On the other hand, Argentina and Australia had sales in all four years. If you use the percentage difference from the table calculations, Tableau uses Table (down), which is incorrect because the rows don't line up (four rows needed for each year

90

for each country). You can quickly fix this by switching it to **Pane (down)**, as shown in step 2. Tableau smartly adds the missing years for each of the countries to correctly calculate the percentage difference. The same result can be achieved using Specific Dimensions (step 3), which you can read out using a mnemonic such as, "For every country, calculate the percentage difference year over year."

Figure 6-15. *YoY calculations by pane and specific dimensions*

One of the most common business KPIs that analysts often calculate for their business review sessions is the infamous WoW (week-over-week comparisons). This mundane calculation could get extremely complicated given the week splits across the years. Let's take the example of the end of the year 2014, containing weeks 52 and 53. You want to complete the week-over-week performance only for those weeks containing the full seven days; otherwise, you would not be comparing apples to apples. There is almost an infinite way of overcoming this. But let's look at two possible approaches based on what you know so far (the Table Calculations and Calculated fields).

Let's start by creating a calculated field to determine incomplete weeks.

$$MIN(DATEPART("weekday",[Order\ Date]))$$

This formula, when dropped after the week of the order date (see Figure 6-16), gives the starting weekday for each row (normally 1 because it corresponds to a Sunday week start by default in Tableau, which you can modify if needed). Knowing this, you can put together the formula to combine Min and Max to get the complete week and flag them appropriately. Week 53 in the example starts on a Sunday but ends on a Wednesday, so it is flagged as an incomplete week.

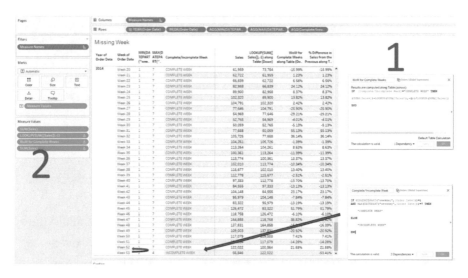

Figure 6-16. *WoW calculations excluding incomplete weeks*

For the first approach, let's use the LOOKUP formula, which brings the value from the preceding or successive rows based on the offset provided (LOOKUP(SUM([Sales]),-1) is the formula to look up one row above). It's then as simple as calculating the percentage difference between the sales of the value and the looked-up value and showing it only for complete weeks.

In the second approach, you use table calculations, which is a lot simpler. You need to choose **Percentage Difference From** and **Table (down)** to effectively calculate week-over-week calculations. You can then choose to hide the incomplete weeks. Please refer to the Missing Week tab in the Tableau workbook corresponding to Chapter 6 for an example of this implementation.

6.3 Sorting

Sometimes the sort yields unexpected results—unless you have a good understanding of the underpinnings of Tableau. When there is a dimension and a measure in the pane, sorting is straightforward. The two sort icons are on the top ribbon. Or, you can specify the sort order by right-clicking the dimension. Let's take a common example of nested dimensions as illustrated in Figure 6-17. The profits are broken down by market and further broken down by category within each market. By default, Tableau displays the markets in the data source order (i.e., their order in the data). Let's fix that by right-clicking **Market** and selecting **Sort**. There are now five options in the **Sort By** drop-down.

- **Data source order** sorts by the initial order in which your data happened to be present in your raw data.

- **Alphabetic** sorts alphabetically. (No surprises here.)

- **Field s**orts by the chosen measure. For example, with profits and sales, you can sort by profits.

- **Manual s**pecifies a custom sort order by manually rearranging the values.

- **Nested**: Specifies the sort order for nested inner dimensions (see section 6.3.1).

For the first market dimension, you can select the field and sort the sum of profits in descending order, and Tableau obediently does so. Also, the market categories need to be sorted; they seem to be out of order. This is covered in the next section.

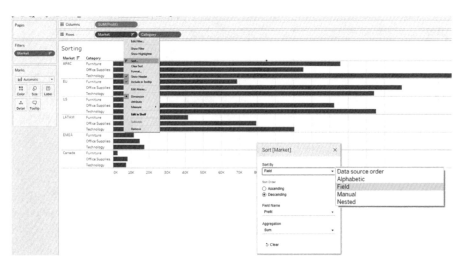

Figure 6-17. *Sorting options*

6.3.1 Nested Sort

Let's sort the categories. You could repeat the steps from earlier and sort using the Field option, but unfortunately, the results are not as expected. The sort order is wrong for markets like the European Union (EU) and Canada. Tableau is first calculating the total profits of the three categories and then determining the sort order for each category irrespective of the other dimensions in the visualization (markets in this case). Technology, office supplies, and furniture form the sort order for the category dimension using profits. Tableau then arranges the category within each market in the same order. In the EU and Canadian markets, office supplies generated more profits than technology, breaking this sort order.

In Tableau, you can specify that the Category field needs to be sorted within each market irrespective of the global category sort order. This is where the Nested option comes to the rescue. Tableau now sorts the category values independently within each market, getting the result you had in mind as illustrated in Figure 6-18.

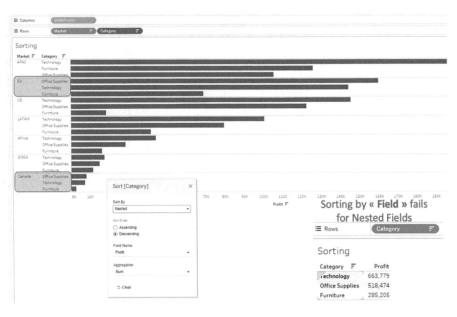

Figure 6-18. *Nested sort*

6.3.2 Rank Sort

Since this chapter is about tables and table calculations, I would be remiss if I did not discuss another rank function option in Tableau. First, drag **SUM(Profit)** onto **Rows** between **Market** and **Category** by setting it to **Discrete**. Now add a table calculation specifying the rank function as the calculation type and **Pane (down)** (or under Specific Dimensions, tick Category), as illustrated in Figure 6-19.

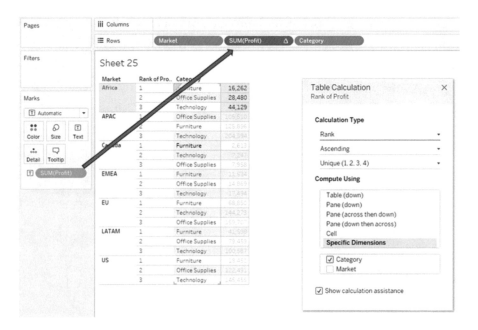

Figure 6-19. *Rank sort*

6.3.3 Sorting in Blended Data

When all your measures and dimensions come from the same data source, Tableau gracefully manages the sorting. But unfortunately, when there is blended data from different data sources, the sorting complexity grows beyond the grasp of Tableau. In these cases, you either do not see the sort option when you right-click the dimension, or even worse, you do see it, but infuriatingly, you don't see the measure you want to sort by in the field name. The workaround for these corner cases is illustrated in Figure 6-20.

Drop the profit measure (secondary data source) onto the rows and set it to Discrete. You can then click the sort icon to force the visualization to use this column as sort (Make sure that you click the pill before clicking the sort icon.) You can then right-click the pill and untick Show **Header** to hide this column from the visualization since its only purpose is to determine the sort order in this example. In the example illustrated in Figure 6-20, you could also directly click the sort icon without moving the profit measure to the rows shelf, which would work since it is already on the text shelf. You need to make sure that it's available somewhere in the sheet.

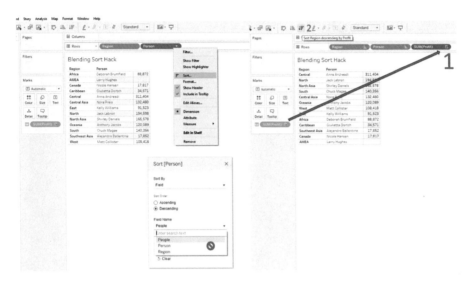

Figure 6-20. *Sorting in blended data*

6.4 Summary

This chapter explained how tables and table calculations could help you replicate the analysis you're accustomed to performing in Excel. The next chapter looks at more advanced topics that add interactivity to analysis with parameters, reference lines, and forecasts, and level of details calculations that perform more advanced aggregations than the default ones provided by Tableau.

CHAPTER 7

Advanced Tips

This chapter dives into a few more aspects that will help you fine-tune your analysis and visualizations.

7.1 Dynamic Inputs Parameters

There were no interactive components in the analyses and visualizations you built so far (i.e., you could not dynamically vary the input values and see the results). This chapter walks through two common use cases. The first one provides the option to dynamically scale up or down the measures. The second one allows you to dynamically vary the measures in the visualization.

Let's imagine you want to present the user with the actual profits by segment while providing the option to dynamically scale up or down the profits. To achieve this, let's start by clicking the down arrow to the right of the search bar on the left pane and select **Create Parameter**. This opens a pop-up window, as shown in step 1 of Figure 7-1. Let's call it **Scaling Factor** and let it take a value between 1 and 50 with a data type of Integer and Allowable Values of Range.

© Shankar Arul 2022
S. Arul, *Tableau for Business Users*, https://doi.org/10.1007/978-1-4842-7786-7_7

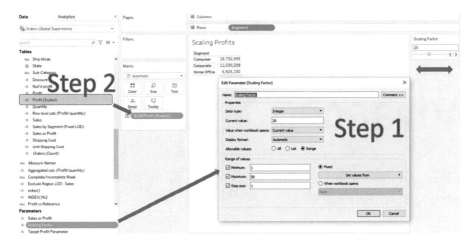

Figure 7-1. *Scaling profits*

You can right-click the parameter and select **Show Parameter**. Moving the scaling factor does not affect your visualizations because you need to wire it up first. In step 2, let's create a calculated field by right-clicking the top of profits. Set the formula to **[Profit]*[Scaling Factor]** and name the column **Scaled Profits**. Now let's add this measure onto the table, and the profits scale up or down as you move the scaling factor parameter.

In the second example, let's increase the heat and try to make dynamic measures. In the dashboards you build, you might want to present the user with an option to select the KPIs that interest the user. This allows you to create lighter dashboards without cramming in too much information and provide flexibility to the end-user.

Let's make a table in which the user can dynamically select either profits or sales. In step 1 of Figure 7-2, let's make the Allowable Values a List, and in the list of values, make sure that 1 and 2 correspond to sales and profit. When you make the parameter visible now, you'll see that it's a drop-down with sales and profit, and each of them internally corresponds to a value of 1 and 2, as defined earlier. Now let's wrap it up by creating a calculated field, in which you specify that if the value of the parameter corresponds to 1, you need to pull in the sales; otherwise, you pull in the profits.

```
IF { [Parameters].[Sales or Profit] = 1 THEN

    [Sales]
```

ELSE

```
    [Profit]
```

END

Figure 7-2. *Dynamic measures*

So, when the user selects profit in the parameter, it internally corresponds to a value of 2, and the formula appropriately fetches the profit measure. Now let's drop it into the table and enjoy the goodness of the dynamic measures.

7.2 Top 10/20/50 Filters

Pareto's 80/20 law says that 80% of the consequences can be attributed to 20% of the causes. In such cases, you want to create quick filters that filter into the top *n* products or items according to your criteria. Let's start by simply creating a Top 5 filter before adding more layers of complexity on top. Figure 7-3 shows a list of products with their associated profits. Drag the product name onto the **Filter** pane, and in the dialog window, the fourth tab is named Top. Select the **By field** option, select **Profits** and **Sum** in the drop-downs, and choose **Top 5** from the **By formula** criteria. This narrows down your list to the top 5 products in terms of profits.

Figure 7-3. *Top 5 filter*

Now let's say you want to filter down into the top 5 products by the country. Drop the Country field into the filter; for demonstration purposes, let's filter into Afghanistan.

The product names disappeared, which is probably not the result you expected. But rest assured, Tableau is doing the right thing, and you try to decipher the logic behind it. In this case, two filters are applied to the same data set: the Top 5 filter on products and the Country filter, which is set to Afghanistan. Tableau has a specific order in which it likes to apply the filters. This is covered at the end of this section. All that you need to know is that the Top 5 filter is applied before the country filter. As a result, Tableau picks out the top five products and then tries to filter into

Afghanistan, and as it turns out, none of the top five products ever made a sale in Afghanistan; hence the table disappears.

The fix for this is to right-click the Country filter and then click the **Add to Context** option. This ensures that the data is first passed through the country filter at the top of the funnel, and the Top 5 filter is successively applied, showing the expected result in Figure 7-4. The filters that are added to the context are highlighted in a brownish-gray color.

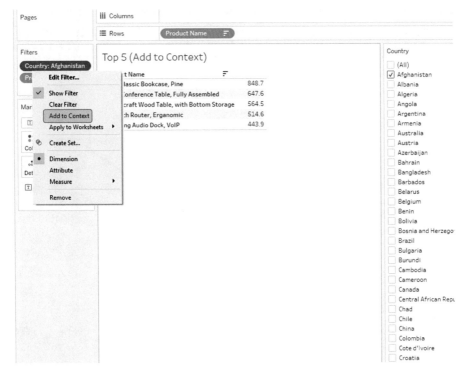

Figure 7-4. *Top 5 add to context*

As is the tradition, let's increase the complexity by adding the dimension of the segment to the analysis. You want to get the top 5 products sold in each segment for the countries chosen. Step 1 of Figure 7-5 shows that the number of products remains at 5; they are not listed in each segment. The fix for this is a little circuitous. You need to add an index() formula to the rows and set the table calculations to increment the products in each segment.

Note   Which dimensions do you untick under the specific dimensions in table calculations. Segment?

Now you can drop the index formula into the **Filter** pane and select the numbers from 1 to 5, which filters the top 5 products for each segment. The country remains in the context, so you know that the data in the visualization has already been filtered.

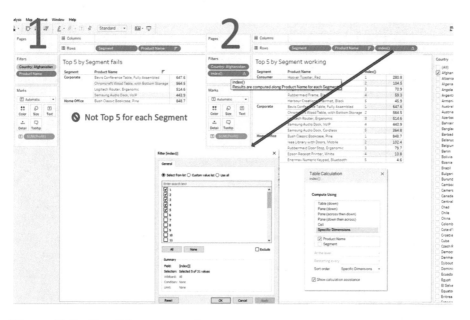

Figure 7-5. *Top 5 by segment*

7.3 Dual Axis

Let's say you want to create a combo graph that includes a bar and a line chart. You could achieve it with the help of the dual-axis graphs.

As highlighted in step 1 of Figure 7-6, right-click the second measure pill. (Note that this doesn't work on the first measure pill.) Select **Dual Axis**.

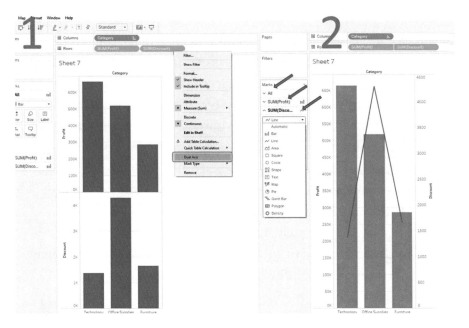

Figure 7-6. *Dual-axis bar and line combo graphs*

In step 2, there are three possible ways to change the visualization of each of the measures. If you choose **All** and set the visualization to **Bar**, it sets both measures.

Since you want to set the discounts on a line, click the **SUM(Discount)** ribbon and set it to Line. Many discounts were offered in the Office Supplies category. Unfortunately, they did not affect the profit numbers compared to the other categories (assuming that a causal link between discounts and profits has been established).

Tableau creates two axes—one for each of the measures. You can force Tableau to use the same axis by right-clicking any axes and selecting a **Synchronize Axis**. In this case, Tableau picks the largest axis and forces it on both. If you synchronize, the profit axis is applied to both, and as a result, you can barely see the discount line.

7.4 Shapes and Icons

Tableau is a data visualization tool, and you need to make your analyses as visual as possible to communicate ideas faster. Tableau offers a palette of built-in icons (or you can create custom icons) that associate with the data. For example, business or financial analysts commonly indicate trends with colored icons. If the trend is positive, an upward-pointing green arrow or a red downward-pointing arrow indicates a decline in numbers.

Figure 7-7 shows year-on-year percentage growth. If the percentage growth is less than 25%, an orange flat arrow is used. If the percentage growth is more than 25%, a green upward arrow is used. With this visualization, you can immediately see that the technology sector is booming in 2014 compared to 2013. Let's start with Figure 7-8, in which you build a simpler version by associating a set of icons to the three different categories.

Figure 7-7. *Custom shapes and icons 1*

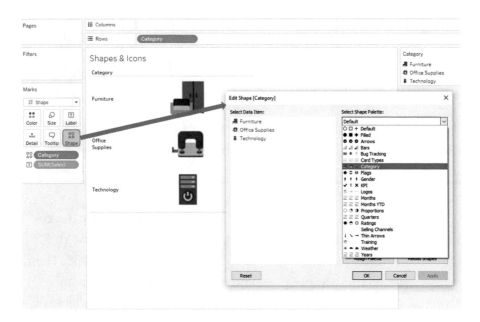

Figure 7-8. *Custom shapes and icons*

Start with a category on the rows and select **Shape** from the visualization drop-down. You'll now see the square appear next to the **Tooltip** pane. Clicking the shape opens a window that allows you to associate any icon with the values in a category.

🌢 CUSTOM ICONS IN TABLEAU

Tableau comes with a palette of icons. You can make your own icons appear in this list by creating a folder in your computer in the Documents ➤ My Tableau repository ➤ Shapes folder and adding the icons, as highlighted in Figure 7-9.

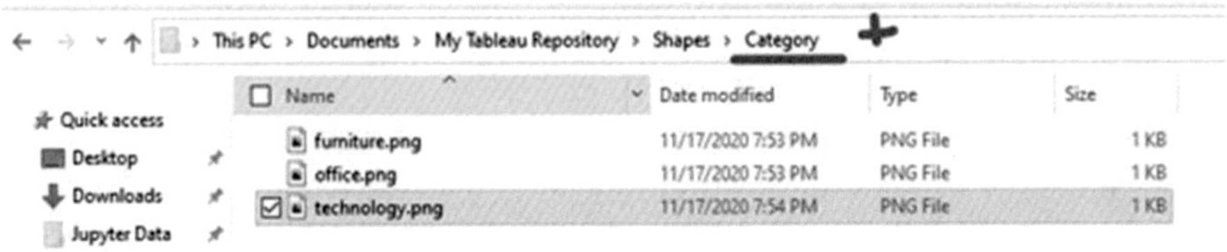

Figure 7-9. *Custom shapes folder*

In case you don't see the folder in your Tableau shapes, make sure to click **Reload Shapes**. On macOS, you'll need to create it at /Documents/My Tableau Repository/Shapes.

To re-create what's shown in Figure 7-7, you need to calculate the YoY calculations for the three categories. First, associate these numeric YoY values to categorical values (<0%, 0–25%, >25%) in a calculated field. Then, drop this field into the **Shapes** pane and associate the right icon with each value. Please refer to the Tableau companion workbook available in GitHub on this implementation (Shapes and Icons 1 tab).

7.5 Level of Detail (LOD) Calculations

Level of details is one of those concepts that take a while to wrap your head around, but once you do, it helps unlock a whole sleuth of advanced analytic capabilities. The good news is that there are three types of LODs to master: FIXED, INCLUDE, and EXCLUDE. Think of LODs as mini tables of data within your data source. This helps you to mash together data with varying levels of granularity.

For most advanced data mashing needs, FIXED LODs get the job done. The general syntax of LODs starts with the keyword, followed by the dimensions that need to be considered. The syntax ends with the measure that needs to be aggregated and preceded by a colon. Figure 7-10 is a schematic representation of the formula.

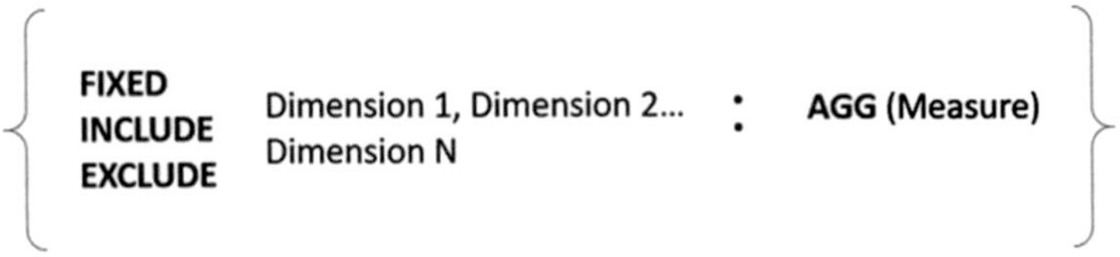

Figure 7-10. *LOD schema*

7.5.1 FIXED LOD

The following is syntax for FIXED LODs.

Syntax: { **FIXED** DIMENSION 1,..N : **AGG**(MEASURE) }
Example: { **FIXED**   [Segment] : **SUM**([Sales]) }

Let's create a new calculated field and call it sales by segment FIXED LOD and use the formula {FIXED[Segment] :SUM([Sales] }. You can imagine the result of this function is a mini table, as shown in Table 7-1. So far in Tableau, when you write a calculated field, you get a single value output, but now, with LODs, it's helpful to think of mini tables, as shown in Figure 7-11.

Table 7-1. *FIXED LOD: Result*

Segment	Sales
Consumer	6 507 949
Corporate	3 824 698
Home Office	2 309 502

For the first illustration, drop the segment along the rows and the newly created calculated field onto the measure and regular sales. The two measures are the same. Why did you have to go through all those hoops if you got the same value? The real power comes when you want to squish the total sales of the segments onto another dimension (i.e., another level of granularity).

Section 1 in Figure 7-11 drops the categories and the order year into two separate analyses (1a and 1b, respectively). The total sales of the three segments repeat on each line of both category and year. Behind the screens, Tableau checks each category/year to determine if the segments are present; if they are, it totals the sum of the corresponding segments to give a single figure of 12,642,502 (the image on the right in section 1). The same total sales value for the segments gets distributed irrespective of category or year.

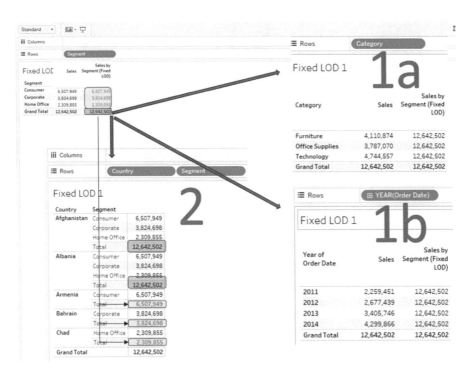

Figure 7-11. *FIXED LOD illustration*

In section 2, let's drop the country and filter into Afghanistan, Albania, Armenia, Bahrain, and Chad to see this in action. Afghanistan and Albania have the same total of 12,642,502 since all three segments had a sale in those countries. For Armenia, for example, only the total consumer sales are pulled in (6,507,949). And for Chad, it's the home office segment sale, which is 2,309,855.

Let's look at the common use case of FIXED LODs in filtering where you want the filter not necessarily to apply to certain dimensions. Figure 7-12 shows the percentage contribution of sales using the FIXED Sales LOD formula and regular sales columns (using table calculations!). No surprise, the percentage split is the same for the two columns when all the years are chosen as the filter.

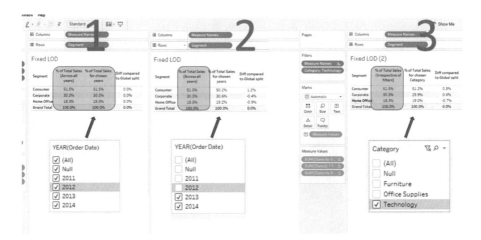

Figure 7-12. *FIXED LOD illustration 1*

In section 2, let's filter in the years 2013 and 2014. The right column using the regular sales is different from the first column using the FIXED LOD, which remains unaltered and shows the same split as in section 1. This is because the regular sales update considers 2013 and 2014 and gives the percentage split across these two years, while the FIXED LOD continues to show the split across the four years irrespective of the filter applied. Section 3 illustrates the same with a filter on the category.

🍏 FIXED LOD AND CONTEXT FILTER INTERACTION

You already briefly looked at context filters, which filter the data upstream before getting to the visualization pane. Let's take another look at it from a different lens and see how they affect LODs. Figure 7-13 shows that by adding the filter to the context, you can constrain the data that gets into the LODs. The FIXED LODs have no effect and mimic the regular sales column in this example. Section 7.7 takes a deeper look at the hierarchy of operations.

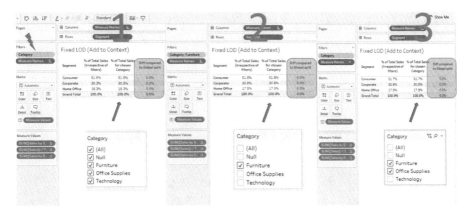

Figure 7-13. *FIXED LOD context filter*

7.5.2 INCLUDE LOD

Syntax: { **INCLUDE** DIMENSION 1,..N : **AGG**(MEASURE) }
Example: { **INCLUDE** [Sub Category] : **SUM**([Sales]) }

The INCLUDE LOD adds an extra level of detail that you specify in your formula and the dimensions in the visualization. To illustrate this, let's look at a tiny data set of nine rows, as shown in Table 7-2.

Table 7-2. *INCLUDE LOD Data set*

Category	Subcategory	Sales
Cat 1	Subcat 1.1	10
Cat 1	Subcat 1.1	10
Cat 1	Subcat 1.2	20
Cat 2	Subcat 2.1	10
Cat 2	Subcat 2.2	20
Cat 2	Subcat 2.3	30

(continued)

113

Table 7-2. (*continued*)

Category	Subcategory	Sales
Cat 3	Subcat 3.1	10
Cat 3	Subcat 3.2	20
Cat 3	Subcat 3.2	20

When you drop in the category along the rows and calculate the average sales, Tableau simply calculates the average of each category group. Since the data set includes three categories with three rows each, Tableau simply averages the values of the three rows for each of the categories. In the INCLUDE LOD formula, let's write it as { INCLUDE Sub Category: SUM(Sales) }. Now let's add this to the visualization and set the aggregation to average. Keep in mind that the visualization contains categories along the rows as highlighted in Figure 7-14. In the LOD, you explicitly said to include subcategories as well in the sum before averaging.

In category 1, there are two distinct subcategories: 1.1 (repeated twice) and 1.2, with values of 10 and 20. Since the LOD includes a subcategory now, Tableau first sums the sales for each subcategory and divides them by the distinct values of subcategories. As a result, it's 20 for subcat 1.1 and 20 for subcat 1.2, which, when averaged, gives 20 for the first line.

In category 2, there are three distinct subcategories. Hence the average is the sum of the three lines divided by 3 (20).

In category 3, you again have two distinct values, so the average of 10 and 30 gives an average of 25.

Tip   In the INCLUDE, try using an average instead of a sum and follow the same logic to see if you understand the aggregations.

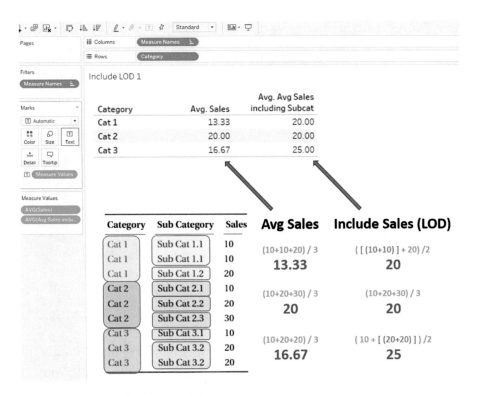

Figure 7-14. *INCLUDE LOD*

7.5.3 EXCLUDE LOD

Syntax: { **EXCLUDE** DIMENSION 1,..N : **AGG**(MEASURE) }
Example: { **EXCLUDE** [Item] : **AVG**([Sales]) }

EXCLUDE does the exact opposite of INCLUDE (thankfully!) in Tableau. It explicitly ignores the dimensions specified in the formula, even if they are present in the visualization. To see this in action, let's make the following sales data set. Let's imagine you opened a blockbuster ecommerce website and managed to sell three orders. For example, in this data set, the person who made the first order bought a handbag, a shoe, and a cap.

Table 7-3. *EXCLUDE LOD Data set*

Category	Subcategory	Sales
Order 1	Handbag	10
Order 1	Shoes	10
Order 1	Cap	20
Order 2	Handbag	10
Order 2	Cap	20
Order 2	Cap	30
Order 3	Shoes	10
Order 3	Shoes	20
Order 3	Cap	20

Now let's say you want to do some in-depth analysis to understand the purchase patterns in this data set of nine rows (sarcastic wink!). You start by dropping the order Ids and the items onto the rows. When you ask Tableau to compute the average, it calculates it at the item level since it's more granular than the order ID. You want to understand the average sales for each order and not at the item level.

It's time for the EXCLUDE LOD to shine. As expected, it ignores the item when calculating the average of each order. Instead, it calculates the averages at the order level and repeats the same value for the items in the same order. This way, you can calculate the Average Item value and Average Order Value in the same table by considering the right level of detail as illustrated in Figure 7-15.

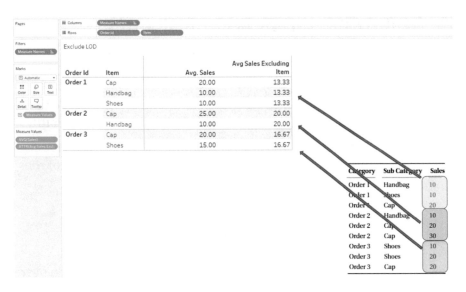

Figure 7-15. *EXCLUDE LOD*

◖ WHEN TO USE LODS

When you are trying to mash together varying levels of granularity on the same visualization, think LODs. The following are pointers to help you get the LOD sense tingling at the right moment.

When you don't want filters to apply to your calculations, use **FIXED LOD**. When you want to calculate averages of distinct groups which are a combination of values across two columns, use **INCLUDE LOD**.

When you want to show the details but want to calculate averages at a higher level of granularity, use **EXCLUDE LOD**.

7.6 Reference Lines and Forecasts

You hardly ever look at a single piece of visualization or analysis in isolation. You are either explicitly comparing it to some expected value or threshold or implicitly comparing it with your mental image of an expectation. Tableau's reference lines come in handy when you want to add a layer of detail (expectation) to your visualization so that you can compare the numbers easily and how they stack against each other or the reference.

7.6.1 Reference Lines Using Parameters

So far, in all the analyses, you remained on the Data tab. Now let's flip over to the Analytics tab and explore the essential ones. Figure 7-16 illustrates the profits broken down by year and category. Imagine the total annual profit expectation for any category could vary anywhere between $50,000 and $200,000. You want to dynamically compare each category against target profits by using red bars if profits are below the reference line and green bars if profits are above it.

First, you need to create a parameter (as highlighted on the right in Figure 7-16) that lists the various scenarios you want to compare; name it **Target Profit Parameter**.

Figure 7-16. *Reference line using parameter*

Tip   If you need to brush up on parameters, please refer to section 7.1.

You then start by dragging the reference line onto the visualization, and Tableau presents a floating pane with three possible options to drop the selection.

- **Table**: Sets the reference line across the entire visualization

- **Pane**: Sets the reference line across each pane for every year in the example

- **Cell**: Appears across each value/cell

Let's drop it on the **Table** option, which then opens another floating window. Under the **Value** drop-down, select **Target Profit Parameter** and close the window. As you slide through the values in the target profit parameter, the line goes up and down, but the bars don't yet change colors if they move above or below the reference line. To do that, let's create a calculated field with the following formula.

119

```
IF { FIXED YEAR([Order Date]),[Category]: SUM([Profit])}
[Target Profit Parameter] > 0 THEN
                "GREEN"
ELSE
            "RED"
END
```

Armed with the knowledge of LODs, you now understand that you're calculating the total profits for each of the combinations of year and category and comparing it against the dynamic target profit parameter. When it's greater than the parameter, green is returned; otherwise, red is returned. The last step is to drop this newly calculated field on the **Color** pane and make the bars change color as you slide up or down the target profits.

Note   Instead of LODs, you could also use SUM(Profit) [Target Profit Parameter], but can you see why you cannot use simply Profit [Target Profit Parameter]?

7.6.2 Reference Lines Using Secondary Data

For example, suppose there are target profits defined by market, and you want to compare the performance of each of the markets against the defined targets. Tableau shows all the measures available in the current data source along with the parameters in the reference line window. So, when you drop the reference line, you cannot choose the target profits in the Value drop-down because it comes from a different data source. The trick here is to drop the target profits on the Detail pane first and then drop the reference line from the Analytics pane onto the visualization, as highlighted in Figure 7-17.

Figure 7-17. *Reference line with secondary targets*

7.6.3 Forecast and Trend Lines

When you need to create quick extrapolations and see them in your visualizations or tables, you could use the **Forecast and Trend Lines** option in the Analytics tab. Do keep in mind that the forecasting option in Tableau is limited to getting directional indicators. The Forecasting window provides options such as the exclusion of periods and seasonality detection.

Figure 7-18. *Forecasts*

7.7 Order of Operations

Tableau has an order in which the filters and calculations trickle down into the visualization. It's crucial to understand the order of operations to ensure that the numbers in your visualization are correct.

Figure 7-19 illustrates that the data flow is from top to bottom. The first filters to get applied are the extract and data source filters that you saw in Chapter 3. Let's focus primarily on the four highlighted boxes as those are the most useful ones starting with the context filters on top of the diagram.

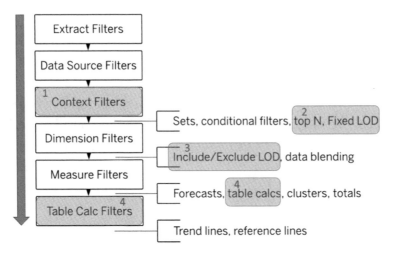

Figure 7-19. *Order of operations*

Section 7.2 explained how to make sure that the top *n* filters work in conjunction with the context filters. To recap, context filters being upstream compared to top *n* ensure that when they are applied, the top numbers are calculated on the filtered data set and not on the global data set.

Section 7.5.1 discussed FIXED LODs and explained how they helped work around the filters in the visualization by fixing the level of aggregation at a different level. Section 7.5.1 also demonstrated that context filters—when applied in tandem with FIXED LODs—get a higher priority, and hence the FIXED LODs get the filtered data and might not work as you might expect. Now you can schematically why that is happening from the order of operations flowchart.

The INCLUDE and EXCLUDE LODs are executed after the filters on the dimension have been applied. As a result, the INCLUDE and EXCLUDE LODs get the filtered data if you have filtered your dimension. Therefore, FIXED LODs get a higher priority/preferential treatment than the other two LODs.

The table calculations are executed at the end, appearing further down the list after all the filtering. So, keep in mind that table calculations essentially manipulate the numbers already visible in your visualization. The Table calc filters are the last of the filters to get applied to the visualization. You can take advantage of this fact and selectively hide and show elements in your visualization without affecting the calculations. Think of Table calc filters as cosmetic filters such as hiding or showing rows and columns in Excel. They have no impact on the calculations.

Figure 7-20 shows that by using Table calc filters, the odd rows are hidden, and as a result, the grand totals on both the tables on the left and the right are the same.

Figure 7-20. *Table calcs run last, and table filters happen even later*

7.8 Summary

This chapter covered advanced functionalities to add interactivity to your analysis, make them more visual with shapes and icons, and squeeze in more advanced calculations with the help of LOD calculations. The order of operations helps you understand the interactivity between the various functionalities of Tableau so that you can build your analysis with full confidence. The next chapter wraps up everything by building a few dashboards so that you can tie all the analyses together and present a more compelling story to your colleagues.

CHAPTER 8

Dashboards

Over the last few chapters, you gained a mastery of Tableau's various analytics capabilities and saw how to effectively slice and dice and visualize your data. Now comes the last part of the challenge: effectively communicating the analyses with your colleagues and the rest of the world. But, to reassure you, this is the easy part of the challenge.

Let's look at how to effectively communicate your visualizations in easily digestible dashboards. If you're part of the new wave of minimalists, you easily understand the concept of less is more. The objective of a dashboard is to communicate the maximum amount of information with the least amount of content. Keeping this in mind, let's get started.

8.1 Dashboards: A 10,000 ft View

The last icon at the bottom pane lets you create a new dashboard (see Figure 8-1). You are not alone if you feel that the empty dashboard and the endless possibilities that it provides are more daunting than understanding the order of operations in Tableau. Block 1 lists all the various sheets and analyses that you have built so far. It's just a matter of tiling them up and applying a brush of makeup to make them look good. Block 2 provides the various placeholders in which you fit your content.

© Shankar Arul 2022
S. Arul, *Tableau for Business Users*, https://doi.org/10.1007/978-1-4842-7786-7_8

Figure 8-1. *Breakdown*

Think of these objects as the framework or the scaffolding that is going to hold your dashboard together. Block 2 also lets you add text and image blocks to your dashboards, among other advanced blocks such as extensions, navigation, and web pages.

Blocks 1 and 2 are present in the Dashboard pane. If you flip onto the Layout pane, you find block 3, which offers dials to fine-tune the size, color, margins, and padding of the placeholders in block 2. With the help of only three blocks, you can start putting together a lot of decent dashboards.

Before starting to flesh out the dashboard, it's always super helpful to sketch out a wireframe of your dashboard and how it should eventually look like. The outline to visually grasp the various elements that you are placed in the dashboard should suffice. Figure 8-2 shows a master dashboard holder highlighted in salmon color (1).

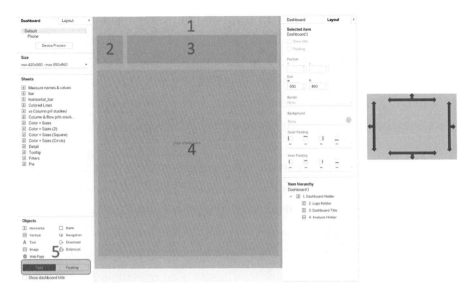

Figure 8-2. *Wireframe*

There are two blue blocks: the one on the left holds the logo (2), and the one on the right houses the dashboard title (3). The green block (4) holds the analysis and visualizations. Now that you know the outline of the dashboard, you can start sliding in the objects from the bottom to start building the placeholders.

Start with a vertical block that houses the entire dashboard, and then drag another vertical block, but this time go toward the top of the dashboard while keeping the vertical block pressed down. As you hover over the top of the block, Tableau visually indicates to you if you want to split the block into two (one on the top and one on the bottom).

Similarly, now take a horizontal block and hover to the top block's right until Tableau indicates that it will horizontally split the top block into two. You can then resize the blocks to make sure they line up the way you want them to. On the bottom of the dashboard in block 5, the **Tiled** option is highlighted. That is essentially what you're indeed trying to achieve (i.e., tiling the blocks to get the wireframe of the dashboard).

Instead, if you select the **Floating** option before sliding in the objects, Tableau allows you to position elements exactly where you want them to be located. It's convenient when you need to fine-tune the position of certain elements but becomes unmanageable if your entire dashboard is composed of floating objects. The recommendation is to opt for the tiled objects over the floating objects, but the choice is yours, and no one can deprive you of that.

In Figure 8-3, on the right in the colored lines visualization, the legend block occupies a lot of space, and you would gain a lot more space by positioning it horizontally. You could do that in two ways. You could click the caret icon (∇) on the block and select **Floating**. This allows you to position the legend block exactly where you need it and stretch it out horizontally.

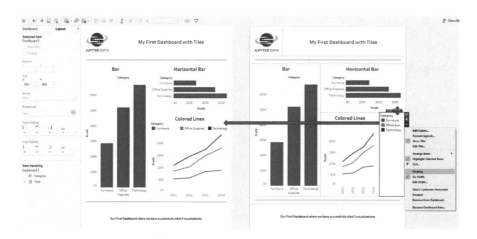

Figure 8-3. *Float certain elements*

Or even better, you could hold it down on the top of the block and move it around. Tableau allows you to snap it in place in any of the blocks, either horizontally or vertically. If you hover over **Arrange items**, you see the option to arrange the values in the legend in various ways within the legend block.

8.2 Fit and Layout

Now that the scaffolding is in place, you need to fit the various objects in the placeholders. Take the example of the first block 1 in Figure 8-4. By default, when you drop a text object in the container, it does not take it up entirely. You need to click the caret symbol and select **Distribute Contents Evenly**. This forces the text element to occupy the entire space and align it centrally.

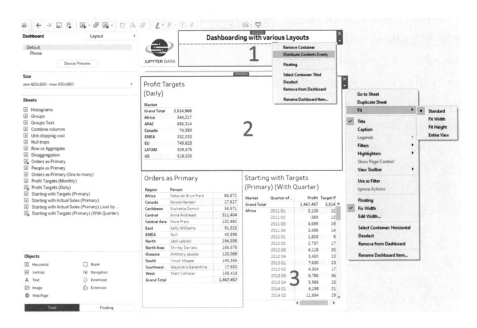

Figure 8-4. *Fit elements*

In block 2, the table occupies the left part of the container. Clicking the caret icon and hovering over the **Fit** option reveals that Tableau uses the **Standard fit** option by default. If you want the table to fill the entire space, you could choose **Entire View**. In block 3, there is a rather long table, and now, if you force it to fit the entire view, the table is illegible as all the rows get squished together. A better option would be to specify **Fit Width**, which makes a vertically scrollable table.

8.3 Filters and Interactions

The real power of dashboards is exposed when you allow your end-users to filter in and out the data. Section 4.1.4 explained how to conditionally filter data in a visualization. If you want to expose these filters in the dashboards, start by clicking the caret and hovering over the **Filters** option. Tableau lists the various dimensions and measures available in this visualization.

In this case, let's expose the segment, quarter, and year of order date as filters. Tableau will drop in the filters in your dashboard, as shown in block 2 of Figure 8-5. Keep in mind that Tableau tends to display the filters within containers that are close to the visualization. As a result, you might have to go on a treasure hunt to find your filters if they get squished in some small container. Even if they are randomly dropped, you know how to move these filters and align them properly using the vertical and horizontal blocks.

As a side note, clicking **Go to Sheet** or the icon highlighted by arrow 1 takes you directly to the corresponding sheet.

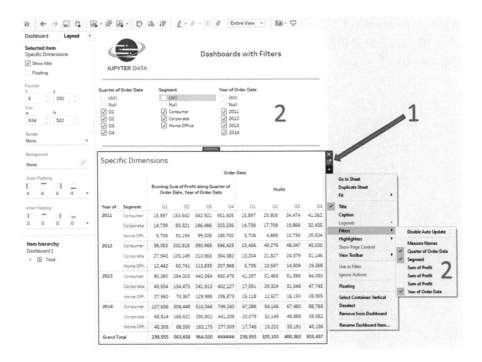

Figure 8-5. *Adding filters*

⬦ FILTERING IN A DASHBOARD

If you need to expose certain dimensions as filters even if they are not present in your visualization, they first need to be added to the sheet as a filter, and only then do you see them on the dashboard when you hover over the Filters option.

8.3.1 Customizing Filters

By default, Tableau displays dimension filters as multiple values (custom list), occupying a lot of space. You can rectify this by clicking your favorite caret icon but this time directly on the filter. In Figure 8-6, block 1 provides a variety of display options. The most appropriate in the case of dimensional filters is the **Multiple Values (dropdown)** option, but the choice is yours.

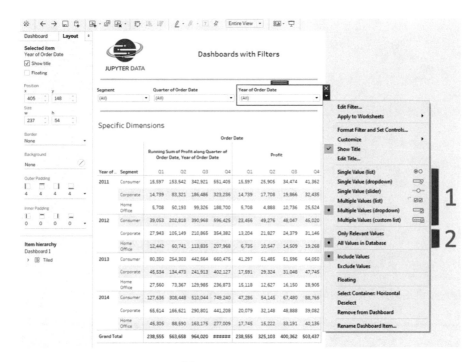

Figure 8-6. *Customizing filters*

You can also choose to show only relevant values instead of all values as in block 2. When you have multiple filters, they come in handy. For example, let's say you have filtered into the year 2011, and it turns out you made a sale in the consumer segment but not in the rest. The segment filter would display the consumer if you chose **Show relevant values**.

8.3.2 Discrete vs. Continuous Filters

Section 3.1 described how Tableau distinguishes discrete and continuous values. As a quick reminder, Tableau uses blue to indicate discrete quantities and green to indicate continuous values. For example, let's say you want your users to filter on the order date in two ways: selecting an individual date or a range of dates with a start and an end date. In this case, you need to drop Order Date into the filter twice, as highlighted in Figure 8-7.

Figure 8-7. *Discrete vs. continuous filters*

Block 1 provides the option to keep the dates as continuous quantities, and block 2 can treat the dates as a discrete quantity. When the dates are considered a discrete quantity, they are drop-down values instead of date ranges.

💣 CHANGING FILTER TYPE FROM DISCRETE TO CONTINUOUS

If you dragged in your filter as a discrete quantity in your sheet, your dashboard does not allow you to display them as continuous quantities. Keep this in mind as you set up your filters as they impact how they can be displayed in your dashboard.

8.3.3 Filter Domain

By default, filters apply on the worksheets that you have applied. Figure 8-8 assembles a dashboard with two visualizations. The one on the left (block 1) uses data blending to combine the orders with the People data set. On the right (block 2) is a simple table with profits by region. Click block 1 and make the Person filter available on the dashboard. When you try to filter specific people, block 1 is filtered, but block 2 shows all regions irrespective of the filter applied.

Figure 8-8. *Filter domain*

To rectify this, you need to click the filter and select **All Using This Data Source**. This ensures that the filter gets propagated to the entire data source, and as a result, block 2 is filtered as well when you apply the filters.

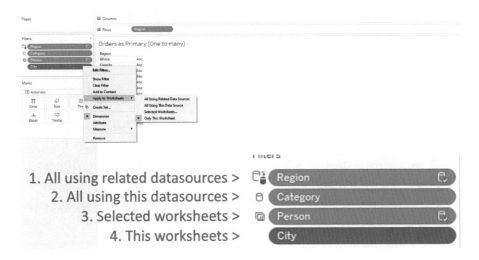

1. All using related datasources >
2. All using this datasources >
3. Selected worksheets >
4. This worksheets >

Figure 8-9. Filtering options

It's much easier to manage all the filter settings on each sheet with the analysis and then display them directly on the dashboard without tinkering too much on the options to avoid confusion as it can easily get out of hand. To summarize, when you right-click a filter in your analysis and choose to **Apply to Worksheets**, there are four options, as highlighted in Figure 8-9.

- **All Using Related Data Sources**: If you're using multiple data sources, this option allows the effect of the filters to propagate to linked data sources.

- **All Using This Data Source**: Restrictive and applies to only the data source concerned.

- **Selected Worksheets**: You can decide to apply your filters on multiple sheets. This filter is highlighted by the superposed sheets of bar graph icon. It can easily slip out of control and lead to unexpected filtering results if you are not meticulous in keeping track of which filters are applied to which sheets if you decide to use this option.

- **Only This Worksheet**: The simplest filter with no associated icons and effects are visible only in the sheet.

Sometimes instead of exposing every possible dimension as a filter, you might be able to provide a more interactive experience to your users by rendering the tables and visualizations themselves as a filter. Figure 8-10 shows how to turn a sheet in a dashboard into a filter. The **Use as Filters** option filters all the values in the dashboard when you click any value in the table. You can identify them on all the sheets where they are applied in the Filters section as "Action (filter name): filter value".

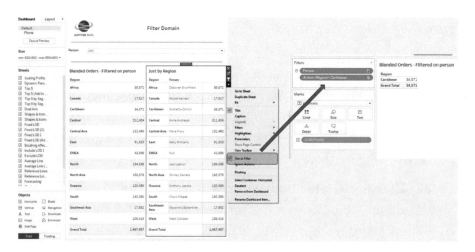

Figure 8-10. *Interactive filtering*

A dashboard ties all your analyses together and presents a coherent snapshot. Story is another tool that you can use in your data storytelling arsenal. Story in Tableau (as in PowerPoint) helps you line up your analysis as slides and walk through them to present a convincing story. As highlighted in Figure 8-11, you can create a new story by clicking the story icon in the right corner. Block 1 lets you add as many story points as you need to communicate your findings. You can then add your analysis from the left to each story point in block 2 and step through them.

Figure 8-11. *Story*

8.4 Summary

In a little over hundred pages, I have tried to distill the essential elements of Tableau and provide the right fishing techniques. Combining the various functionalities in Tableau offers countless options. But, if you understand the base elements and their functional logic, you can mix and match them confidently and draw data analytic conclusions with confidence. I wish you all the best, and Godspeed on your quest to master Tableau!

Index

A

Aggregations, 25, 26, 57, 58
Anscombe's data set, 2, 3

B

Big data, 1
Business questions, 21, 23

C

Calculated fields
    calculated columns, 55, 56
    definition, 55
    null values, 56, 57
Cardinality
    approaches, 68
    blending relationships, 67
    Global Superstore v1.xlsx
        file, 67
    issues, 69, 70
    left joins, 70
    market level, 69
    market/order date, 68
    Orders table, 66
    target profits, 68
    target table, 69

Columns and Rows shelves
    bar chart, 28, 29
    Cartesian product, 30
    categories, 30
    dimensions/measures, 30
    flipped horizontal bar, 30
    stacking, 31
    total profits, 28
Custom color palettes, 35

D

Dashboards, 49
    Blocks, 125–127
    creation, 125, 126
    filtering, 131
    floating, 128
    wireframe, 126, 127
Data analytics, 1
Data modeling
    Data Source tab, 71
    logical *vs.* physical layer, 72
    Market and Order Date/Order
        Daily, 71
    relationships *vs.* joins *vs.*
        blends, 73
    Targets table, 71

S

Shapes and icons, 106, 108

Sheets, 48, 49

Show Me button, 47, 48

Sneaky pie chart, 46, 47

Sorting

    blended data, 96, 97

    nested sort, 94, 95

    options, 93, 94

    rank sort, 95, 96

Stories, 49, 50

T, U, V, W, X, Y, Z

Table

    scratch, 77

    Show Me, 75, 76

    tips, 76

    totals, 78

Tableau Public

    download page, 7, 8

    import data, 9, 10

    installation, 7

    Microsoft Excel, 9

    profile page, 8

    site, 7

    version, 7, 8

Table calculations

    approaches, 92

    calculated field, 92

    down then across/across then down, 84, 85

    formulation, 89

    month over month (MoM), 90

    pane, 83

    reading, English, 86, 88

    table

        across, 81, 82

        down, 80, 81

    visualization, 79, 80

    week-over-week (WoW), 91, 92

    year over year (YoY)

        pane/specific dimensions, 90, 91

        pitfalls/workarounds, 90

Tabular data, 18

Top 10/20/50 Filters, 101, 103, 104

Printed in the United States
by Baker & Taylor Publisher Services